SOFTWARE ENGINEERING EXPLAINED

Mark Norris and **Peter Rigby**
BT, UK

JOHN WILEY & SONS
Chichester · New York · Brisbane · Toronto · Singapore

Other Wiley Editorial Offices

John Wiley & Sons, Inc., 605 Third Avenue,
New York, NY 10158-0012, USA

Jacaranda Wiley Ltd, G.P.O. Box 859, Brisbane,
Queensland 4001, Australia

John Wiley & Sons (Canada) Ltd, 22 Worcester Road,
Rexdale, Ontario M9W 1L1, Canada

John Wiley & Sons (SEA) Pte Ltd, 37 Jalan Pemimpin #05-04,
Block B, Union Industrial Building, Singapore 2057

Library of Congress Cataloguing-in-Publication Data

Norris, Mark.
  Software engineering explained / Mark Norris, Peter Rigby.
    p. cm.
  Includes bibliographical references and index.
  ISBN 0 471 92950 6
  1. Software engineering.   I. Rigby, Peter.   II. Title.
005. 1—dc20   91–44133
                                                CIP

British Library Cataloguing in Publication Data

A catalogue record for this book is available from the British Library

ISBN 0 471 92950 6

Typeset in 10/12pt Palatino from author's disks by Text Processing Department,
John Wiley & Sons Ltd, Chichester
Printed and bound in Great Britain by Courier International, East Kilbride

SOFTWARE ENGINEERING EXPLAINED

Contents

Preface

This book aims to introduce and explain some of the more important aspects of modern software development. It is not a detailed guide to any one part of the software development process, nor is it a reference manual for the software engineer. There are many excellent texts listed at the end of the book with more detail in specific areas . This is meant to be an overview of basic good practice in the specification design and operation of quality software.

Some chapters of the book are designed to stand alone—for instance the middle chapters (4 to 7) each deal with one major part of the software development process and are supported by a catalogue of techniques and a checklist to help their implementation. The book as a whole, though, is designed primarily as a source of information rather than a software reference manual.

The intended readership is fairly broad. Our aim was to write a primer for people with no formal background in software whose jobs have become dominated by it. In addition to this, the practical bias of the information here would be of use both to managers of software projects and to students about to embark on a career in software.

Above all, we hope it is interesting, useful to dip into, but mainly fun to read.

We would like to thank several people whose co-operation and forebearance have helped with this book.

Malcolm Payne for his constructive review of the initial drafts and his continual encouragement. Bob Higham for his careful reading of the completed text. Debbie Legassie for converting our hieroglyphics into English (American) text... and always with a smile on her face. To our many friends and colleagues in BT Software Development and Technology divisions whose experience and advice has been invaluable, especially Ray Lewis, Sinclair Stockman, John Foster, Dave Bustard, David Horncastle, Trevor Matthews and Jonathan Mitchener. Last, but not least, our wives, Fiona and Liz, for their forebearance, patience and support throughout.

M. Norris
P. Rigby

Foreword

Software, or rather the ability to produce it, is now recognised as the key to competitive advantage in a high technology business. This book is a guide for those who want to win that advantage. It is not theoretical—there are already many excellent textbooks that address those aspects of software engineering.

The book aims to highlight the key concerns that have to be addressed by anyone involved in the development of software-dominated systems. For each of these concerns the book explains the current state of the art, what the known pitfalls are and what tools and techniques are available to help.

The book brings modern software engineering techniques to professionals who are working in the software industry. This does not mean to say that it looks solely at the software engineering professional—many engineering professionals wish to adopt software engineering as a second string to their bow.

A second category of audience for this book is those undergraduates who are intending to take up a career in the commercial software field, as it introduces the techniques required to scale theory into practice.

Before we look at the possible solutions that this book may offer, it is interesting to spend a few minutes reflecting on the nature of software itself. It is characterised by the fact that the whole product is documentation in one form or another. Indeed, in many instances, it is just a very long piece of program text, generated with no concept of how it can be broken down into configuration items and subsequently rebuilt to form the product.

The principle of structured software, that each portion is simple to understand and modify, is crucial. This can only be achieved in software—the product—if the process by which it is produced is well founded. The main part of this book therefore addresses the main process steps in producing reliable, long-lived software, from requirements capture, through to maintenance and eventual retirement.

At the end of the day, whatever the software application and however it is defined, its objective is to instruct a machine to do a certain specified operation. It must be able to do this operation time and time and time again, without fail, to the satisfaction of the people who are using it. The important point that has emerged in software development over the last few years is that the creation and support of a system is a demanding intellectual process. This book brings together several years of experience and investigation into the process, and I would like to think that reading it will save the reader from reinventing the wheel, and more especially from coming up with a square one without giving thought to the option of rounding the corners.

A.G. Stoddart

1

Why Software Matters

There are only two commodities that will count in the 1990s.
One is oil and the other is software. And there are
alternatives to oil

Bruce Bond

Software engineering is all about producing what the customer wants within time and cost constraints. A quality product to do this requires a mix of technical and organisational skills. That is what this book is all about. Later chapters look at some of the important tools and techniques that can be used in developing a software system. Before we start, though, there is an important question that needs to be answered:

Does software quality really matter that much?

There is no straightforward answer to the question but there are ways of gaining some insight on it. The first is in terms of the damage that can be wreaked by faulty software, the second is simply based on the cost of producing and maintaining software. The next two sections give a few examples of the importance of software quality from the 'catastrophe' and 'cost' perspectives. The reader is left to assess the relevance of the examples in their own environment.

1.1 SOFTWARE FAILURES

For obvious reasons, the developers and owners of software systems—especially those in safety or life-critical areas—are usually unwilling to discuss failures which have occurred. Nevertheless, some notable instances of failure have been recorded and they provide valuable evidence of the critical need for software quality.

Radiotherapy equipment

A radiotherapy machine was designed to operate in two different modes. In the first mode, the machine delivered a low dosage of radiation; in the second mode, the machine delivered a much higher dosage to a smaller area, with a mask in place to screen the rest of the patient. In the reported incident, the high dosage was given, without the mask in place, and the patient died.

According to the inquest, the control system for the radiotherapy machine was a software-controlled replacement for an earlier hardwired version. In the earlier version of the machine, there was a safety interlock which prevented the high dosage unless the mask was positively in place; it appears that the software version of the system lacked this interlock.

Misguided torpedo

A conference on safety and security of software systems featured a report on the safety system in a torpedo that was designed to prevent it returning in error to destroy the ship which had launched it. It achieved this by detecting that the torpedo had turned through 180° and was threatening its source. If this was the case, it was automatically detonated before it could return to do harm.

Unfortunately, when the torpedo was being tested, it was launched with a live warhead, but its motor failed and this left the live torpedo lodged in the torpedo tube. The ship's captain decided to abandon the test and return to port. As soon as the ship was turned round, the torpedo did its duty and exploded in the tube.

Autoland system

A prototype automatic plane landing system was designed to work in two stages. In stage 1 the plane flew down a beam which determined the approach path. If the plane lost the beam, the system applied power and flew the plane around for a retry. In stage 2 a ground detector sensed that the plane was within a few feet of the ground, cut the engine and raised the nose to land the plane. In separate testing both systems worked perfectly.

In the first live test, both systems again worked perfectly. The plane flew down the beam until the second system detected that it was near the ground, then the engine cut back, the nose was raised, and the plane started to sink. Then it lost the beam. The engine was boosted to high power and the nose was lowered by the first system. Before the second system cut back in, the plane flew into the ground.

A similar system, developed a few years later, demonstrates a less dramatic but no less serious problem. In this instance, as before, the software worked perfectly. During tests the plane landed every time with unerring accuracy. After a few weeks, however, revision of the system (i.e. rework of the software) was required, not because of malfunction but because the test runway was beginning to break up where the plane unfailingly alighted.

This second example illustrates an important point. Despite the fact that not all system failures are the fault of the software, it is the system element that is, almost invariably, changed to cope with such unforseen circumstances as described above.

Chemical plant

The specification to the programmers stated that, if an error was detected, they should keep all controlled variables constant and sound an alarm. The programmers were not chemical engineers.

In the reported incident, the system received a signal from an oil sump that the oil level was low. In accordance with the specification, the system stopped changing any values and issued an operator alarm. By coincidence, the system had just released a catalyst into the reactor and was in the process of increasing the water flow to the condenser. The water flow was held at a low level, the reactor overheated and the pressure release valve vented a quantity of noxious fumes into the atmosphere. Meanwhile the operators investigated the alarm, discovered that the oil level was actually correct, and did not notice the reactor overheating.

None of these examples are exceptional. In fact they appear to be fairly reproducible. A recent report of a high-speed-train braking system revealed that the prototype implementation was designed to operate in one mode up to 50 mph and in a second mode above 50 mph. Unfortunately, attempts to stop the train when it was travelling at precisely 50 mph were fruitless as neither mode of braking would operate at this speed. The problem, in essence, was the same as the first of the autoland incidents described earlier.

The reason for revisiting these sad cases here is simply to illustrate the fragile divide between satisfactory operation and disaster.

In order to learn from these mistakes, it is important to examine the root causes of failure—missing requirements, a misunderstanding of the function of the system, and the like. A point that will come up several times in this book is that software quality is not simply a matter of well structured code or accurate design. It relies on a systematic approach that covers the entire system development and allows inconsistencies to be revealed [Hil88].

Returning to the original question of whether software quality matters, there are many applications that rely to some extent on software, from nuclear reactors to fly-by-wire passenger aircraft to banking systems. Failure as described above could be catastrophic in any of them It would be unrealistic to expect perfection on every occasion but the value of eradicating any error should be clear.

1.2 SOFTWARE COSTS

To some people, money is almost as emotive an issue as life itself. For that select band (and for the information of everyone else), there are some interesting figures that show just how much software costs now and is likely to cost in years to come.

Before going into detail, a few trends taken from a number of the strategic reports published [ACA86] highlight the central importance of software to all companies involved in any form of information technology. Some of the more striking points made are:

- Software currently accounts for about 5% of the UK gross national product and, given the trends over the last ten years (shown in Figure 1.1a), this is likely to grow.

- The proportion of IT costs attributable to software rose from 40% in 1980 to 80% in 1990 (see Figure 1.1b).

- The European software services market, estimated at 40BEcu in 1990, is set to rise to more than 60BEcu by 1993.

In addition to these gross-size figures, these strategic reports have identified a number of key problems, the main ones being [Hob90]:

- On average, large software systems are delivered a year behind schedule.

- Only 1% of major software projects finish on time, to budget.

- 25% of all software-intensive projects never finish at all.

- Over 60% of IT product managers have little or no experience of modern software engineering practice.

The effects of the above factors have been estimated, in cost terms, to be of the order of two billion pounds a year in the UK alone. The overall picture is of a costly area of technology, growing rapidly in which failures are rife.

So far we have set the general environment and trends. To give a better feel for the actual scale of investment in software, we can look at a 'typical' small software company. Since there is no apparent source of reproducible information on industrial software productivity, the line taken is to state what is known, or can be reasonably assumed and to derive a reasonable overall picture.

Assumptions

(a) There are about 100 engineers in the company involved with software development and maintenance.

(b) The split of effort on development and maintenance is 47:53. This figure is an average across a number of software maintenance surveys and accords reasonably well with published data from the US.

(c) In terms of lines of code (loc), the average for development is about 20 loc/person/day. For maintenance an average programmer load is about 17 000 loc/person/pa. The former is a guess based on hearsay and experience, the latter is from published data.

Observations

(a) Given the number of software engineers engaged on maintenance, 53, and the amount that each can maintain, we can derive that there are about 900 Kloc deployed at any one time.

(b) The other 47 engineers must be developing code at a rate of 20 loc/day for 45 weeks in a year. This equates to around 210 Kloc of new code a year. There are a number of factors that come into play at this point: the amount of code taken out of service (about 90 Kloc every year, assuming an average lifetime of 10 years); the attrition rate of projects (if 25% never complete, only about 155 Kloc are usefully added every year; 90 Kloc replacement, 65 Kloc new).

(c) Taking the example figures used above, our small company increases the amount of software deployed by 65 Kloc per annum. This rise of just over 8% equates quite closely with the general trend for increasing proportions of software in systems (but ignores any increase in the number of systems, so is probably on the low side).

For all their subjectivity, the above figures are not at all unexpected—they are reasonably in line with common experience and can be backed up with published material. There are two key points that emerge:

- That if our small company had to replace its entire software base, it would, by any standards, be a costly exercise.

- The annual bill for software development and maintenance is large (simply based on the volume of code) and is growing.

Both of these points indicate that the cost of poor quality is potentially high: if a software product is not fit for its purpose it can become more of a liability than an asset [Boe88].

One final point that needs to be considered in answering the question of whether software quality matters is that of liability. It is likely that, in future, suppliers of software systems will be accountable for the sort of failures

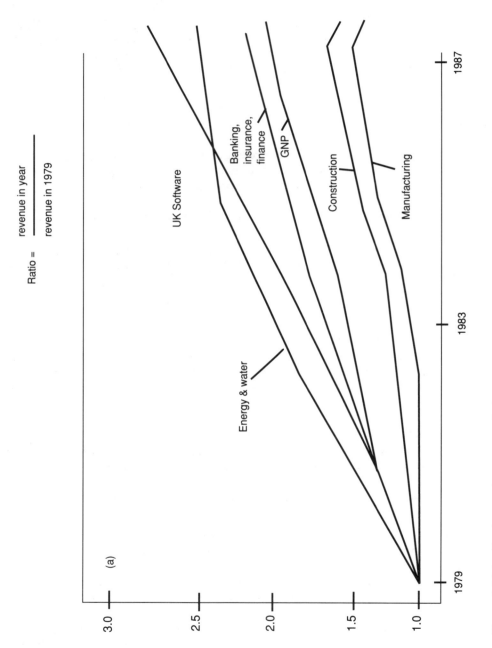

Figure 1.1(a)   The increasing economic importance of software through the 1980s in the UK

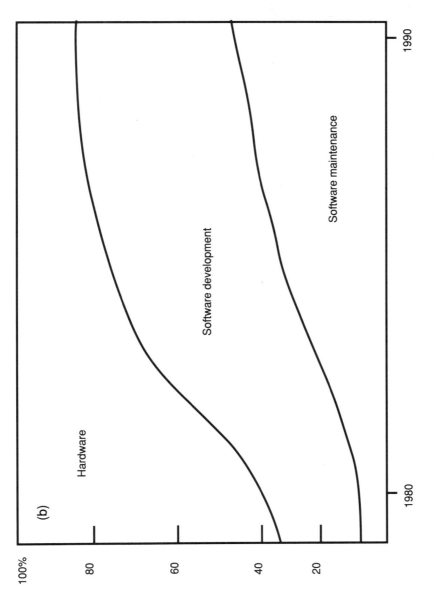

Figure 1.1(b)   The increasing dominance of software as a system component

illustrated at the beginning of this chapter. In Europe it is already the case that due care and attention has to be shown by the supplier. The prospect of law suits could well introduce a new clarity to the costs of failure!

Overall, it would seem that there is more than sufficient cause for concern over the quality of software, both in terms of safety and cost. The question now is what can be done to achieve 'quality'.

Before this can be answered, we have to define what we mean by 'quality'. As far as the end user is concerned quality is fitness for purpose and can be viewed as a combination of a number of 'desirable features'. The provision of the required level of functionality is obviously crucial in this—the software must do what the user wants. There are a number of other attributes that differentiate good quality software; its performance, reliability, usability, etc. and it is often these attributes that have most impact [Hig90]. A user may be able to tolerate the lack of a particular function but poor system response or unreliability may lead to total rejection of the system. The user's perception of quality is based on the following types of system features.

- *Reliability.* Good-quality software systems should not crash every time exceptional loads or data are applied. The increasing dependence on (networked) software systems is driving expectation of higher levels of reliability.

- *Security.* This covers both confidentiality and access rights. Again, greater dependence on software systems is driving the need for their protection.

- *Adaptability.* Software needs to be amenable to change. If it cannot be readily updated to meet changing market/legislative needs then it will rapidly fall into disuse.

- *Performance.* Users expect to work at interactive speeds. Response times must match this need.

- *Usability.* This includes ease of use, ease of learning, presentation and attractiveness. A far greater level of user adaptability is expected in modern systems.

The above list is far from exhaustive but it does provide a basis for what software systems really need to deliver if they are to satisfy end users [FII89]. Figure 1.2 indicates how some of these quality factors can be related to user needs.

The achievement of quality as defined in user terms is far from easy. If there was, this book could be reduced to a short pamphlet. The problem is that quality in the above terms is only achieved by ensuring that a whole range of technical and organisational issues are adequately addressed by the supplier. And there is no formula or recipe to ensure that the tools and techniques used to produce the software will result in what the user really wanted.

User Needs	User Concern	System Requirements
Functional	How secure is it?	SECURITY
	How often will it fail?	RELIABILITY
	How easy is it to learn?	USABILITY
Fit for purpose	How efficient is it?	PERFORMANCE
	Does it interface easily?	ADAPTABILITY
	Is the software easy to operate?	USABILITY
Flexible	How easy is it to repair?	MAINTAINABILITY
	How easy is it to change?	ADAPTABILITY
	Is it reusable in other systems?	REUSABILITY

Figure 1.2   Some links between user needs and system requirements

Some of the main contributors to software quality from the supplier's viewpoint are explained in later chapters. For now though we aim to provide a little insight as to the nature of software quality .

Perhaps the first point here is to differentiate between the quality of the software itself (the product) and the way in which it is produced (the process). This may appear to be a spurious separation as the product is part of the process: tangible evidence of its completion. In quality terms, however, the two are distinct and need to be examined in isolation.

1.3   QUALITY ASSURANCE

The current approach to the Quality Assurance (QA) of software is to specify a set of procedures which define the various operations in the development that are to be achieved, such as the format and naming conventions for documentation, coding standards, review procedures, etc. This introduces some basic stability into the software development process; the general rule being:

- Write down what you are doing.

- Do it.

- Prove that you are doing it.

This is the approach that underpins all of the current software quality assurance registration standards such as BS 5750, ISO 9000 and AQAP [RSN89]. Any organisation which obtains registration or approval to these standards (or has a scheme of equivalent calibre) is deemed to have achieved a basic level of control over what it produces. Unfortunately this approach leaves a lot to be desired in a number of respects.

- The set of procedures which guide the operation of the organisation put few constraints on what is actually produced. They simply provide a framework for its production.

- The procedures must specify 'how' to do a task, but do not have to specify 'why'! If procedures appear irrelevant, there is little chance of any commitment to them.

- Following on from the above point, the quality assurance team are often seen as pedants producing spurious bureaucracy and not helping the designer to produce a better end product.

In fairness to the approach it offers one over-riding advantage. It provides a common basis for development, an essential precursor for measuring and improving the process.

Once a standard approach to a task is installed it becomes possible to record statistics and to determine some basis for overall improvement (e.g. by identifying common problem areas). Before the impact of this discipline can be realised, however, the procedures must evolve and this whole evolution can be defined in terms of a number of key stages in 'quality maturity':

- *Anarchy.* No systematic control of any part of the process—there is freedom to do whatever is expedient.

- *Stability (Quality Assurance).* This brings some order out of chaos and provides a core process for software development. In some cases there is no justification other than the belief that 'it will feel better'.

- *Measurement and Control (Quality Control).* Measurement can only be achieved in a stable environment where what is being measured is identifiable, repeatable and quantifiable. Measurement enables control.

- *Improve (Quality Improvement).* No real-world process is perfect, so improvements, based on observation of current practice, are always possible.

- *Theory (Quality by Design).* Once a process is well understood, underlying theories that explain cause and effect develop.

The relationship between the above stages is illustrated in Figure 1.3 which shows a basis for the evolution of any scientific method. Software engineering is currently far from the stage of having established theories but stable processes do exist and the measurement loop can be entered. This is the first step which takes us from Art to Craft and then from Craft to Science (albeit soft science). Although we have touched on a step by step way to move software quality forward (and this is revisited in the latter chapters of the book), the first step must be to introduce stability into the development process.

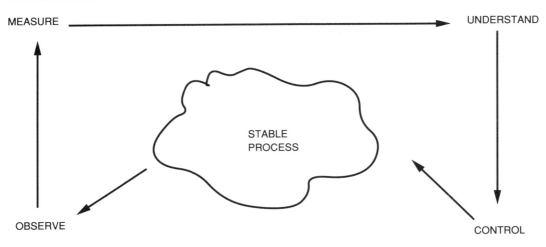

Figure 1.3 How the quality improvement process works

1.4 QUALITY CONTROL

To explain the need for control in software development, it is worth first looking at how it applies in other areas.

The military possibly provide the best example of strict control. When an order is given to do something all of the individuals receiving the order do it the same way. The advent of military discipline can be traced back as far as the Romans, who were prime exponents of the art. They showed time and time again that a smaller force, better trained and disciplined, frequently defeated larger forces of rabble. A less rigid example of control can be found in many team sports where individuals work to a plan devised to help their team win, rather than follow their own ideas. But how does this equate with software quality?

The 'hacker' approach to software relies on the initiative of the individual. Given brilliant individuals brilliant products can, then result, but given the general level of most practitioners the standard result is usually poor. Recent reports indicate that Japanese software houses, by their disciplined approach, have caught up with and are now surpassing the Americans in terms of the quality of the software they produce. The error rates and the productivity that they now achieve are superior to those reported in the USA and this is primarily attributable to the more rigorous application of defined procedures.

Thus again control is proving to be the better route than unconstrained freedom. In this context, the basis for control is that all the practitioners use the same techniques and tools in similar areas, enabling information to be shared and understood by the whole team.

The introduction of a structured approach to software development is a first step in quality control. It introduces a defined process with checkpoints for assessing quality at intermediate stages of the process (e.g. design reviews, code walkthroughs, etc.) and allows the process to be stopped at any stage for remedial action. There is a long way to go before quality is guaranteed, however. Once control is established, the next step has to be improvement of the process.

1.5　QUALITY IMPROVEMENT

An improvement programme relies on modifying a process based on observation and measurement of how it currently performs. A common approach to improving software development processes at present is to use defect data from operational systems and to relate this to the way in which the system was originally developed. The simple collation of fault reports, for instance, can reveal a great deal about where errors are found (e.g. crucial modules or 'hot spots' within the high-level code) and when they are introduced (during specification, testing, etc.).

A number of recent reports have shown how a quality improvement programme can identify and correct development errors. To complete the picture, there is now a considerable body of evidence to suggest that improvements in process quality do have a significant effect on the quality of the end product. Figure 1.4 shows a comparison of two similar projects, one with installed quality procedures, the other without. The beneficial effects are clear.

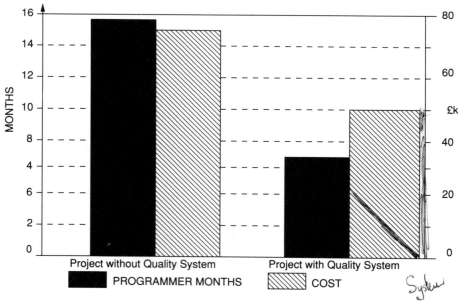

Figure 1.4　The difference quality has on productivity for similar projects [Hob90]

The link between the software development process and the product that comes out at the end of it is not, however, a simple one. A poor process can produce good results just as a good process can produce rubbish (albeit less frequently). Quality improvement ensures visibility and testability during development. The final step in software quality has to concentrate on the product itself, though. Designing quality in, rather than painting it on later.

1.6   QUALITY BY DESIGN

Ultimately, software quality should not be achieved by continual corrections. It should be designed in from the very start. The process should be so well understood that no defects at all are introduced once the first valid representation of the system (e.g. the specification of requirements) has been produced.

Ideally, we should like to be able to gain a clear and unambiguous statement of what is required, analyse this statement to ensure that it contains no errors and then transform it into an executable form that performs exactly as intended under all circumstances.

At the present time this is something of a distant aim. Given the current lack of 'software theory' (i.e. the standard measures and specific laws that underpin a science) quality by design can only really be based on observation and experiment. Later chapters of this book aim to explain what constitutes good practice in software development. This may not ensure quality by design but it does provide a reasonable start in that direction [Mon89].

There are four key areas that we consider here as crucial stages in achieving quality by design. These are:

- *Requirements.* These are frequently far from clear and often change during the development of the system. Small mistakes at this stage can lead to major problems.

- *Design.* Systematic design techniques can focus the efforts of teams of developers working on a project and can help to expose potential problems before they are implemented.

- *Testing.* Significant errors are often found in software the first time it is used. With a little planning, a great number of potential problems can be removed during test.

- *Maintenance.* Given that software systems inevitably have to change to accommodate changing requirements, it is important to establish a safe and well controlled mechanism for updating.

Before moving on to these essentially technical topics, though, we consider in some detail the nature of software and the various ways in which its development can be approached. Figure 1.5 shows how the above areas

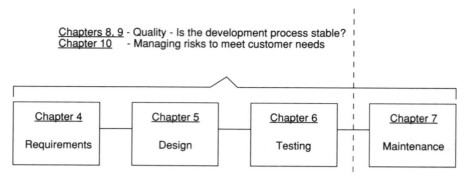

Figure 1.5 How the chapters in this book fit together

fit together with reference to the structure of this book. Despite the emphasis on measurement so far, there is no chapter on the subject. This is not an oversight, more a reflection of an important requirement as yet unfulfilled by adequate theory or standards. Practical measures are introduced where appropriate throughout the text.

1.7 SUMMARY

Software quality is undoubtedly important. Lack of it can result, at best, in considerable financial loss; at worse, in unsafe or insecure products being released on an unsuspecting user. Improving software quality is already important and may, one day in the not too distant future, be a legal obligation.

The question of how to guarantee software quality is, however, a complex one.

This chapter has introduced the key stages in achieving software quality from anarchy, where there is freedom to do whatever the designer wants, through stability, control and measurement to a stage where the achievement of quality can be planned.

The current best industrial practice is not yet at the stage of 'quality by design', however. Quality assurance—usually achieved through control over the development process using established standards such as ISO 9000—is increasingly prevalent (and required) throughout the software industry. A guide to some of the current standards for quality assurance is given towards the end of this book.

Given the importance of software systems, our main concern should be *product* quality assurance and this implies control over the technical evolution of the software itself as well as the development process. The remainder of the book examines the key technical and organisational aspects that contribute to software quality.

1.8   REFERENCES

[ACA86] Software—A vital key to UK competitiveness (1986) *UK Cabinet Office report*.

[Boe88] Boehm, B. (1988) *Software Engineering Economics* (Prentice Hall).

[FII89] *Future impact of information technology* (1989) (*BCS Trends in IT Series*). (British Computer Society).

[Hig90] Higham, R. *et al* (1990) Technology prediction in software engineering *Proc. Software Engineering '90 Conference* (Brighton) (IEE).

[Hil88] Hill, J. (1988) The development of high reliability software—RR&A's experience for safety-critical systems *Proc. Software Engineering '88 Conference* (Liverpool, 1988).

[Hob90] Hobday, J. (1990) Opening address *Software Engineering 90 Conference* (Brighton, 1990) (IEE).

[Mon89] Monk, P. (1989) *Technological Change in the Information Economy* (Pinter Publishers).

[RSN89] Rigby, P., Stoddart, A. and Norris, M. (1989) Assuring quality in software—practical experience of attaining ISO 9001 *BT Engineering Journal* **8.4**.

2
Characteristics of Software

Between the idea and the reality, between the motion and the act,
Falls the shadow

T.S. Eliot

In the last chapter we gave a few examples of software-based projects that went wrong. There are many more such examples. This chapter starts to explore *why* those accidents happened. We now start looking in a little more detail at what it is that we are trying to engineer quality into—the software itself.

This is no straightforward matter as software is different things to different people and so defies a simple definition. For instance, the user of a system may regard the software as no more than a collection of programs and data that make a general-purpose computer into a special-purpose machine designed to perform a particular application. Given this definition, the main concerns would be to ensure that a complete and compatible set of programs and data is used. An alternative definition from a software developer's point of view might be that software is all of the information (i.e. documentation) produced during the development of a software-intensive system. The connotations of this definition are very different to the user's view. Issues such as validation of the specification and verification of the implementation are raised and the structure of the information required to produce the user's compatible set of programs and data to perform a particular application becomes the focus of attention.

The above definitions are two out of many, each of which highlight important aspects—some practical, some theoretical—of the development of quality software. To understand the relevance of these various aspects we need to explore the nature of software, to look at its characteristics and some of the known problem areas. Once the problem has been defined and put into context we can begin to suggest how it should be developed.

2.1   SOME GENERAL DEFINTIONS

Software is characterised by the fact that the *whole* product is documentation (indeed, it could be a single text). Some of this is purely explanatory, some is for the benefit of the user, some supports the installer, some is for the reference of the maintainer [Fre87]. The 'working' part of any software-based product (i.e the high-level code) is also text—it is distinguished by the fact that it is written in a sufficiently formal way that it can be used to command a machine to perform specific functions.

Each part of this documentation set (usually) takes a different form—software representations include programs written in high-level code, detailed designs written in a software description language, architectural designs in the form of structure or data flow diagrams, specifications written using formal notations, system requirements expressed, typically, in natural language, and so on. In short, all of the information that impacts on the eventual set of programs and their associated data can be considered to be a valid part of a software representation and hence of 'the software' itself.

For each of these representations of software there are numerous languages and notations which can be used. Figure 2.1 gives some idea of the range of languages that can be used to direct a computer to carry out a required set of actions. At the lowest level, a stream of 0s and 1s (machine code) drives the computer directly. At a slightly more abstract level, assembly language can be used to manipulate processor operations. High-level languages are further removed from the actual machine operations and require intermediate devices (such as compilers) to relate code to the actions it specifies.

The complexity of many systems make it impossible to write code before a considerable amount of thought has first been put into design and requirements, and these activities also have their own languages. For instance, system requirements can be expressed in natural language, they can be captured pictorially using a method such as Soft Systems Method (SSM) and they can be presented as a series of tables and viewpoints with the COntrolled Requirements Expression (CORE) method. There are many other ways of making the capture of user requirements systematic, although this is probably the least well served stage of the software development process: the number of high-level programming languages commercially available now runs into hundreds.

In some ways the richness of available representations is useful in that it allows appropriate representation of the problems in hand. For instance, the standard Specification and Description Language (SDL) and its associated high-level programming language, CHILL, have been specifically developed for, respectively, the definition and implementation of telecommunications switching systems. The choice of an appropriate representation is often not so straightforward, though, and requires considerable thought. This is an issue covered in some detail in subsequent chapters dealing with the main phases of software development.

1st Generation   **MACHINE CODE**

                                                   10101110 10010001

2nd Generation   **ASSEMBLER**

                                                   8085, Z80, 68000, etc.

3rd Generation   **HIGH-LEVEL LANGUAGE**

                                           Procedural (line by line instructions)
                                                   Pascal   CORAL 66
                                                   BASIC   etc.
                                             Declarative (state the problem)
                                                   LISP   Hope
                                                   PROLOG   (FORTH)
                                               Object-Oriented (models)
                                               SMALLTALK   C++   EIFFEL

4th Generation   **DATA BASED (not real time)**

                                                       CICS
                                                       SQL

5th Generation   **ARTIFICIAL INTELLIGENCE AND**
                                               PARALLEL PROCESSING

Figure 2.1   The range of languages for software systems

The selection of a consistent set of representations is currently one of the primary issues facing software development professionals and the organisations for which they work. It is one of the troubling realities, however, that other considerations such as time limitations or predetermined operating constraints often cause this important factor to be relegated to a low priority.

Although difficult to demonstrate, the impact of inadequate representations can readily be seen as an underlying cause of some of the software failures described earlier. A specific example of this would be the first of the autoland systems described in Chapter 1. The fact that a key interface (that between the two guidance beams) was not highlighted as vital, indicates that the representation of the problem was probably inadequate.

A second important definition that needs to be made is for 'quality' [KW86]. Software quality (in the broadest terms) has already been defined as software that performs to meet the customer's requirements. This definition holds right through the lifetime of a software product—it must conform to customer needs when delivered and must continue to do so until it is superseded.

There are two important points that follow from this definition:

● Quality software must not only work—it must also do what the user wanted it to do.

● It must be amenable to change.

The first of these points is illustrated in the second part of the autoland example described earlier. The software produced to do the job operated exactly as specified. Unfortunately it did not fulfil the customer's real requirement (which was to land the plane but not destroy the runway)! The importance of accurate requirements is highlighted by a study of software systems carried out by the US Department of Defense. The results of this study, shown in Figure 2.2, indicate that 'building the right system' is as important as 'building the system right'.

Even after the right system is built, it will (assuming that it is useful) have to change as new functions are required, interfaces are changed and data is altered. The implication here is that systems must be built to cope with

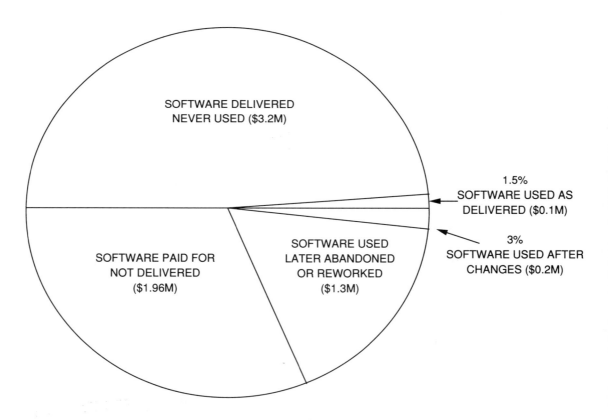

Figure 2.2   Usability of software contracted by US DoD

these inevitable changes, i.e. they must be designed to be easily maintained. The 'maintainability' of a software system is difficult to define but its absence is readily seen. A benefits payment system designed only a few years ago required costly modification to cope with its first cheque of more than $99.99. A simple change was all that was required: the location of the required changes, however, took considerable time and effort.

The sensitivity of software to change can be illustrated (rather dramatically) by a list of the world's most expensive programming errors, kept by Gerald Weinberg, which records the cost of fixing one-line changes to operational software systems. Many of the entries run to millions of dollars and, although no details of the errors are given, the message is clear: software that is not readily maintainable is more of a liability than an asset.

2.2 COMPLEXITY

Until relatively recently, software was something that was added on after the main part of the system, the hardware, was built. This is a reasonable approach when the software requirements of the system are well defined and fairly straightforward, but can lead to severe problems if features of the hardware are inappropriate to the system constraints and have to be compensated for in the design of the software.

The impact of this potential problem can readily be illustrated by looking at the approximate size (and probable complexity) of software in modern systems. Figure 2.3 shows the approximate size of a number of software systems in terms of the length of printer paper it would take to list them. The details are sensitive to debate and change but the general point is that software systems are growing very large, especially when compared with human limits of comprehension.

Software systems comprising several million lines of code are not rare. The increasing need for distributed and networked systems with greater functionality will inevitably increase the number of such systems. At the same time, increased reliance on software sytems will drive expectations of more reliable systems [NJ87].

Given the trends towards increasingly complex systems with more stringent reliability requirements, hardware considerations should not drive the development process in the belief that they are the dominant cost and most inflexible design element; while they may be, one cannot really confirm that without looking at the overall system.

The question of whether a particular function or task *should* be implemented in hardware or software is a red herring; neither is the right approach because only with a systems approach that takes into account and evaluates both elements appropriately can a system be produced that meets the functional and operational requirements of the customer. The system approach is an essential part of developing software systems and this implies that more abstraction is required.

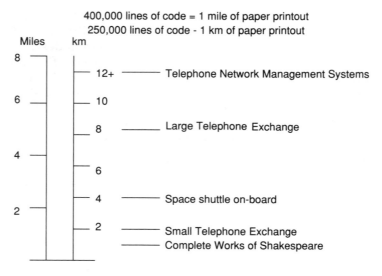

Figure 2.3   An illustration of the relative sizes of software systems (Foster's metric)

Often, the choice of hardware/software split in a system is dictated by what is already available. This can be seen in the move towards standard platforms—Unix is now a *de facto* standard operating system that provides a common set of services and interfaces for applications, giving portability of applications software. In addition, the Open Systems Interconnect (OSI) standards provided through the International Standards Organisation (ISO) give a sound basis for interoperability between software from different vendors. Both provide a reliable base upon which to build new systems. Economics dictate the use of these standard platforms and they provide the virtual machine upon which new software is built.

The detail will always be there and will always matter but the only way to cope with complexity is to abstract and this is happening both with the increasing use of platforms such as Unix and with the adoption of design techniques that support abstraction.

2.3   PROGRAMS AND DATA

The application for which software is being produced often has a significant impact on its structure and organisation. Two application areas that typify this are 'real-time' systems such as network switches and 'data processing' systems such as airline reservation databases. The first type of development might well be implemented in the C language, specified in terms of finite-state machines or as an object-oriented design and hosted on a Unix machine. The second would more likely use COBOL as the high-level language, be specified in terms of entity-relationship diagrams and use MVS as the operating system.

On the face of it, these differences are not particularly important but they do highlight one of the often overlooked characteristics of software: that it is comprised of both programs and data. Neither can be ignored.

The distinction can be difficult to make in some cases. For instance, is the data in a large database, software? Generally, the database itself is viewed as being outside the realm of software (but certainly not outside the realm of computer science, nor of systematic ways of building the collection of data) while the data that define a database and its access is a part of the software. The impact of ignoring this can undo even the best plans. A few years ago one of us ran a project aimed at developing software design techniques. One of the cornerstones of the project was a method of manipulating finite-state machines (commonly used to represent the control flow in a program), allowing the designer to compare them, check for differences, etc. The algorithm developed to automate the task was elegantly derived from the theory of finite-state machines and implemented as a set of matrices. The trouble was that the algorithm required successive matrix multiplication to yield results and, in practical application, they were very sparse and for anything other than trivial problems, grew very large. Had the data been taken into account at an earlier stage, a different implementation would have been chosen. It could not have run slower than the one that was actually developed.

2.4   MEASUREMENT

The measure used earlier in this chapter to illustrate the complexity of modern software was lines of code. This is a commonly used measure of software but its use needs to be carefully considered. There are many ways of measuring software—size, complexity, usability—but the correlation between these measures and the quality of the software is tenuous. Effective information can really only be generated by using several sources of data. For instance, to establish a meaningful measure of maintainability, it would make sense to record attributes of the software, such as complexity, along with process measures, such as fault report data. A correlation of these two could indicate where the problem modules are in the system. Taken independently, the measures convey little useful information.

This is the case with one of the most common misconceptions in the software field—that productivity can be measured by how many lines of code are produced in unit time. This focus can condition the entire environment to concentrate on the production of code. The result, time and again, is the production of mountains of code that cannot be integrated to work as an efficient system (if at all), or the building of a system which does not satisfy the needs of the customer even though it may work well technically.

Although still immature, the measurement of software and the process of its production is viable [STR90]. In practice, it is often the simple measures, such as the maintainability measure outlined here, that provide the necessary information to understand and improve quality.

2.5   THE 'LAWS OF SOFTWARE'

Unfortunately, there are no laws of software in the same sense as there are laws of rugby. Even so there is a body of received wisdom built up over the last 30 years that applies to all large software projects [Leh80]:

1. *Software does not wear out.* Although this may be true in principle, it certainly does not accord with reality. Very few of the software systems created twenty or thirty years ago are still in operation. Lines of code are very easy to change, but systems can be incredibly difficult to alter successfully. This comes about because of the underlying fact that software is a system with thousands of interwoven dependencies and interconnections. Consumers' requirements continually change and, rather like old cars, keeping old software can be an expensive and fairly exclusive pastime.

2. *Change is inevitable.* Software must be designed to be maintainable. To survive it must be built as though it will continue far beyond the retirement of its creators, will be adapted to run on new equipment, enhanced with new functions, repaired to take care of those pesky special cases, and generally outlive those that created it. There are obvious counter examples—truly one-shot situations, applications for equipment that is about to die, functions that are eventually outmoded—but it is better to err on the side of too much preparation for the future rather than too little.

   Much good information about the structural aspects of a piece of software is lost during development. Initially, this may not pose a problem, but eventually it usually does since this is precisely the information that is needed to help preserve the integrity of the software during evolution (typically called maintenance, although it incorporates three kinds of change: repair, adaptation, and enhancement). This is similar to an organisation that divides itself into departments and then loses all information about which employees belong to which departments; reorganization will be very difficult.

3. *Maintenance makes software better.* Every time that a change is made in a piece of software, there is a finite possibility of new errors being introduced. The net effect of maintenance *may* be to improve the software; it may make matters worse. The latter is more likely to be true if, for instance, inadequate documentation is kept or if no change management procedures are implemented. It has been established that structural information (definition of sub-units such as modules and the interfaces between them) is essential for maintaining technical and managerial control of a software system as it undergoes change over time. In spite of a wave of techniques incorporating 'structure' in their names (programming, design, analysis, testing), it is still common to find software produced with little attention paid to its physical structure and even more

common to find that, after initial development, no coherent record of the system's internal structure is maintained.

4. *The real cost of software ownership is low.* If the cost of maintaining the software is not made explicit, then the perceived cost of ownership is low. Taking maintenance to mean all corrective work carried out after delivery, the actual cost can be high.

   Software of any magnitude costs quite a bit to create in the first place (and, worse, it usually cannot be considered a capital cost). If it has been used very much, then quite likely considerable money has been spent on it over the years to repair, adapt, and enhance it with new functions; it is not uncommon to find that three or four times the original development cost has been spent in this way.

5. *Software never dies.* Taking a more appropriate definition of quality as meeting customers' *perceived* needs, then software that cannot be economically maintained to meet these needs is dead. This is a reality that many people and organisations learned years ago. Yet because the average length of experience of people in the field seems to be dropping (due to the rapid expansion of the use of computers and hence of people's involvement in creating software) it is a lesson that people constantly learn anew the hard way!

   Software lives forever for any number of reasons, good and bad. The most obvious and pervasive reason is that once built and in productive usage, there is inertia that must be overcome if it is to be changed or replaced. The users like it. The boss likes it. The customers like it. It doesn't matter that it is slow, prone to errors, needs to be expanded to take care of new functions, and so on. The software has become a part of their lives and all they want is that it be fixed up a bit—certainly not replaced or changed in any major way!

6. *Size does not matter.* As the complexity of a software project rises, so does the difficulty in producing a satisfactory product. There are limits (albeit arbitrary) beyond which conventional techniques of development and management have yet to go. Behind these limits, there are also distinct break points in software project size—it is often the case in practice that doubling the size of a project team has little effect on timescales, etc. [Bro75]. Figure 2.4 suggests some current limits and size categories in software development.

The relationship between software and the people around it (users, customers, managers, operators, and so on) is not unlike the relationship between people who find themselves associated for historical reasons (e.g. in a marriage, working situation) which may have little bearing on their present situation. It takes a tremendous amount of effort to change

(a)

Total size:	10 million lines
Number of major components:	1000
Component size:	10,000 lines
Design Life:	10 years
Project Team:	100 staff
Quality:	1 error per 10,000 lines
Productivity:	50 lines per day/programmer
Rate of repair:	1 day per fault per 1000 lines
Fault rate:	1 fault per 10,000 lines

Figure 2.4(a)   Approximate limits in software

(b)

Category	Number of programmers	Duration	Product size
Trivial	<1	1–4 wk	Up to 1K source lines
Small	1–2	1–6 mo	1K–5K
Medium	2–5	1–2 yr	5K–50K
Large	5–50	2–3 yr	50K–500K
Very large	50–200	3–5 yr	500K – 5M
Extremely large	200+	5–10 yr	5M+

Figure 2.4(b)   Appropriate size categories for software development

the situation and break the relationship to the software! The result is that the software lives on and on.

2.6   FUTURE NEEDS

So far, we have outlined some of the key characteristics of existing software systems. One final characteristic that needs to be considered before moving on is what the forces for changes are. The next decade is likely to be one of significant changes in the area of software engineering [RC89]. As we move towards a more engineering-based approach to software development in the mid and late 1990s, so there will be an increased skill requirement for our development staff and the focus of software development activity will move steadily away from implementation to design. In addition, there is likely to be an increasing emphasis on automation of the software process.

All of these trends are characteristic of a move away from a quality control approach to software development, towards a quality improvement and quality by design approach. Whilst this holds out many opportunities for the European software industry, it also holds out many threats which must be faced if we are to survive and prosper beyond the year 2000.

The first threat is the sheer volume of software we are producing in our progress towards an information society. We are increasingly reliant upon software-controlled systems for the information upon which we make our decisions, should they be personal, commercial or administrative. All this clearly indicates that we cannot afford to stand still with respect to the quality of our software development processes.

Factors driving the need to improve include:

- Increased complexity of the systems we are developing.

- Rapidly changing requirements.

- Increased functionality of requirements.

- More stringent non-functional requirements such as usability and maintainability.

- Higher reliability requirements.

and, ultimately

- Commercial survival.

This last point is not included just for dramatic effect—84% of companies who have a fire in their computer room fold within four years of the fire. The above list provides high-level goals for what needs to be done in terms of improving software quality. These overall goals now need to be linked through to the technical and procedural development that can enable them to be achieved.

2.7 SUMMARY

Clearly software is many things. It is different things over time, different things to different people, and different things depending on what you intend to do with it. This is not really surprising. Anything that is complex is not only open to many interpretations but should be viewed in different ways for different purposes. The important point is that the right view for the task at hand needs to be selected.

In this chapter we have tried to guide this choice by outlining some of the important characteristics of software that should be considered:

- There are many different ways of representing software. There is plenty of choice but the problem is in determining an appropriate and cohesive set.

- Software is growing increasingly complex. To cope with this, a major trend in the software industry is towards more standardisation of both platforms (e.g. Unix) and applications (e.g. OSI conformant systems). The impact on the software designer is that it is the intellectual process, leading to the creation and evolution of high-level code, which is of critical importance.

- Software consists of both data and programs. There is a tendency to focus on one or the other. Both matter and need to be considered.

- Software can be measured but it is the interpretation of the measures that really counts. The commonly quoted measure of 'lines of code' is meaningless until it is related in some reproducible way to other aspects of the software it is trying to describe (e.g. do more lines of code imply poorer maintainability?).

In addition to these characteristics, there are a number of widely recognised 'laws of software' that encapsulate the experience of many successful (and some failed) software development projects, such as that change is inevitable, maintenance makes software better, etc. The truth (or otherwise) of these laws is discussed in this chapter.

The objective of this chapter has been to give a feel for the nature of software and what the important aspects of software development are, both now and in the future. In all cases we have relied on observation of practice rather than explanation of theory since the foundations of software as an engineering discipline are, as only to be expected given its relative immaturity, still evolving.

2.8   REFERENCES

[Bro75] Brooks, F.P. (1975) *The Mythical Man-Month: Essays on Software Engineering* (Addison Wesley).

[Fre87] Freeman, P. (1987) *Software Perspectives* (Addison Wesley).

[KW86] Kitchenham, B.A. and Walker, J.G. (1986) The meaning of quality, *Proc. Software Engineering '86, Conference* (Southampton) (Peter Peregrinus).

[Leh80] Lehman, M. (1980) Programs, lifecycles and laws of software evolution *Proc. IEEE* pp1060–1076.

[NJ87] Norris, M. and Jackson, L. (1987) An engineering approach to system design *Proceedings of Globecom 87 Conference* (Tokyo).

[RC89] Raghaven, S. & Chand, D. , Diffusing software engineering methods *IEEE Software* **6.4** (July 1989).

[STR90] Stockman, S., Todd, A. and Robinson, G. (1990) A framework for software quality measurement *IEEE Journal on Selected Areas of Communication* **3.2** (February 1990).

3

The Evolution of Software Systems

A mighty maze but not without a plan
Alexander Pope

An organised approach to software development is essential. There are many opportunities to make mistakes from misconstrued requirements right the way through to an incorrect implementation. The complexity of modern software systems means that their development has to be broken down if it is to be manageable. This chapter explains some of the frameworks that have been used to describe and manage software developments

There are numerous models of the software development process currently available. These vary in nature from purely descriptive (they simply describe what exists) to prescriptive (they state what steps must be taken).

Since we are dealing with models, rather than reality, each has its own area of usefulness. There is no one 'right' model for all purposes and no model is complete as all abstract in some way from the details of reality. Even so, the use of a suitable model can help considerably in the control of a software project. Figure 3.1 is an example of what such a model looks like.

In this diagram the problem-oriented aspects of design (in which the real world is involved, on the left-hand side) are distinguished from the design-oriented aspects (in which abstract modelling is paramount, on the right-hand side). This is, however, only one of many ways of describing the various activities that are involved in development. The main purpose of the diagram is not to illustrate any deep point but to introduce the concept of what is termed the software 'lifecycle'. The next few sections go into some detail on what is available and how it can be applied.

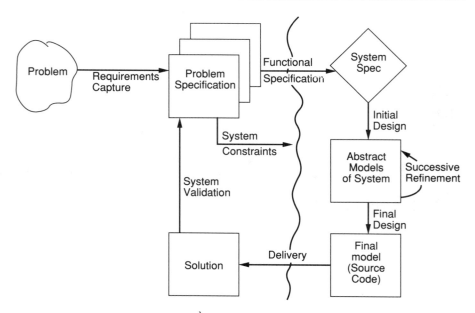

Figure 3.1   Overview of the activities in system development

3.1   THE SOFTWARE LIFECYCLE

The lifecycle provides a convenient model which serves two purposes. Firstly, it allows one to represent the process of conception and production in a graphical and logical form and, secondly, it provides a framework around which quality assurance activities can be built in a purposeful and disciplined manner [Ago88].

The development of software from initial concept through to operation is an evolutionary process. That is to say, it is produced through successive stages of specification, design and modification. Each assessment of a piece of software, be it by a review of the documentation describing requirements, specification, design or, later, by tests on the code and field use of the released system, results in changes. Ideally, the development process should involve successive tiers of specification and design where each step is verified against the requirements of the preceding stage. Thus a viable software product is evolved with errors being found and corrected as they occur.

The most commonly used model of software development, illustrated in Figure 3.2, is often called the 'waterfall or V model' (probably because of its similarity to a set of cascading waterfalls). It depicts the software lifecycle as a set of linked but discrete activities with inputs downwards to successive stages and feedback upwards to provide verification against previous stages and a final validation of the requirements.

Although by no means a perfect representation of what really happens, this model has been in widespread use for some 15 years now. It is explained

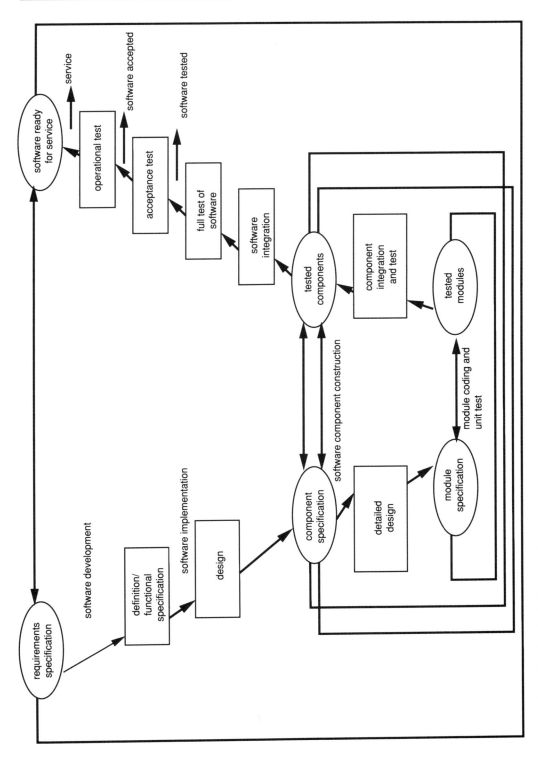

Figure 3.2   The 'waterfall' lifecycle

in some detail here to give a feel for what a lifecycle model describes and how it can help in controlling the software development process.

The first stage in this model is the definition of requirements. This is invariably the first stage of any problem-oriented process and is in many cases the most difficult to achieve. The next chapter explores the reasons behind this . For now we will simply state that the problem lies in the communication between customer and developer. The former are not always in a position to define precisely what is required and, as a result, the latter usually have great difficulty in producing a specification in sufficient detail to allow accurate translation from the requirements into the design. Even in cases where the customer and designer construct a precise set of requirements the very act of developing the system tends to result in a modification of the customer's original perception of what the final need is. The requirements stage can be compared with the preparation of a legal document. The more precise it becomes, the more difficult it is to understand. If precision is omitted, then the scope for ambiguity and misunderstanding increases.

Assuming, for the moment, that a satisfactory set of requirements can be drawn up, there is a basis for the next stage in the waterfall model. This takes us into design and usually requires the developer to respond to the stated requirements with some form of functional specification which defines the externally apparent functions of the system as the developer perceives them. The various options for tackling this equally important stage are outlined in Chapter 5. The material output from this stage is a definition of what the developer plans to implement, thus providing the first visible evidence to the customer that the eventual product will be what was ordered.

From here on, in the waterfall, one becomes involved in design iteration of some form. At the highest level a system design is established which will allow the separation of software components from non-software components and the definition of the interface between them. Very often an architectural design will be generated in order to establish a framework. Software design is then performed by use of an established 'top-down' methodology. It is here that the greatest effect on quality can be seen since the quality of the design will, to a large extent, determine the final quality of the product. The lowest level of the software design will provide the basis for coding and will largely define the structure of the programs. In the iterations through the design the overall problem should be sufficiently broken down to leave only minor difficulties for the programmer. In practice this is rarely the case and some design decisions taken at an early stage are not implementable. In such cases it is then necessary to resort to redesign and iteration until the problem is solved.

The next major stage in the waterfall is concerned with the testing of the coded design. This activity takes place at various levels. At the lowest level programmers must debug their own source code in isolation from other parts of the system. Once consistent within themselves, tested modules can be presented for integration to the system of which they are part. As inte-

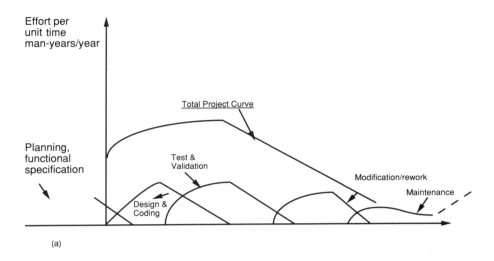

(a)

Figure 3.3(a)   Phasing of activities through a software development

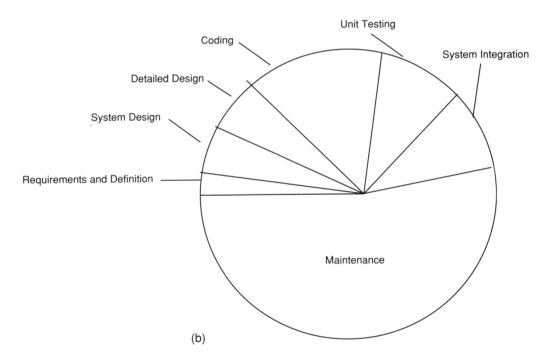

(b)

Figure 3.3(b)   Typical proportion of activities over a software product life

gration progresses and external functions begin to appear the customer can be provided with the opportunity to view the potential product. This can prove invaluable in demonstrating both that the system is being developed as originally specified and also to detect points of misunderstanding in interpreting the original requirement.

Acceptance testing usually concentrates on demonstrating the functional aspects of the product. In reality it is delivery and operation which usually reveal the degree to which the product meets the customer's requirements. A detailed account of the techniques for software testing is given in Chapter 6.

Finally an acceptance test of the completed system will take place before its release. At this stage the customer may 'sign-off' the system, possibly with some defects still acknowledged. That is, however, far from the whole story. It is essential that the post-release evolution of the system be considered as part of the system lifecycle, right up to the point of obsolescence. Typically, software systems spend longer in service than in development (e.g. telephone switching software has a design life of 20 years). Inevitably alterations are required to the released system, both to correct errors found in the field and to add new functionality to the system.

The ongoing maintenance activity, whereby faulty or missing requirements are revealed and addressed and new requirements are added, needs to be considered as part of the overall software lifecycle. This is covered in depth in Chapter 7.

The time spent in each of the above lifecycle phases varies from project to project. Figure 3.3 gives some representative figures, both for the proportion of effort on the activities and for their phasing.

The waterfall lifecycle model is not the only one available. It has, however, the advantage of being the most commonly used and hence the best understood. The main benefit of adopting this model lies in the fact that the opportunities for feedback within it are many and thus, provided that the system developer wishes, the propagation of faults can be largely prevented by the detection and verification activities at each stage.

There are of course a number of deficiencies in the waterfall model: the distribution of activities is not sequential, as described, it does not acknowledge development through prototyping, etc. Nonetheless it has been applied successfully in very large and complex projects, such as the System X switching system, and is still in widespread use.

3.2 MORE LIFECYCLES

As observed above, the waterfall model is by no means the only way to view software development [KF81]. For all its uses it pays little regard to inevitable parallelism of actual projects and it focuses on procedural activities rather than costs, etc. Although there are many approaches to modelling software development, the selected examples in this section serve to illustrate the diversity of what is available.

The evolutionary lifecycle

This model recognises the need for regular review of a development as it progresses and as requirements, etc. inevitably change. The evolutionary lifecycle is usually represented by a 'spiral' (or snail) model, as shown in Figure 3.4. This shows a development as a stepwise, incremental process rather than a sequence of compartmentalised phases.

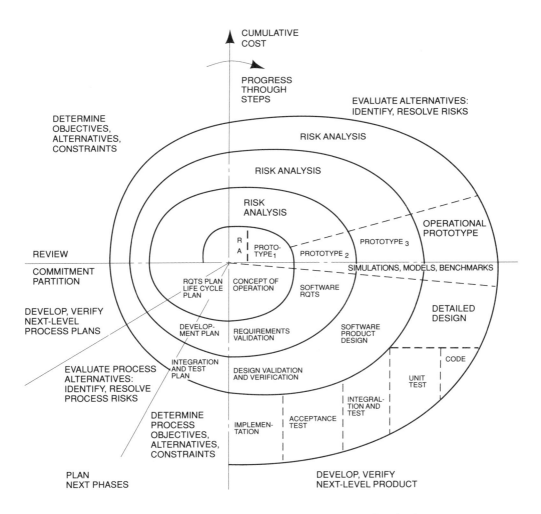

Figure 3.4   The spiral model of software development (after Boehm)

Using the model, each increment of work passes through the following stages:

1. A review of perceived objectives.

2. Assessment of the risks for each of the options for the next stage of work.

3. Plan for development of chosen option.

4. Development.

5. Review of deliverables from the stage to check that they meet initial objectives.

The main advantage of adopting this lifecycle is that it allows a considerable amount of flexibility in a project. On the negative side, it calls for constant attention and does not readily admit longer-term plans. Nonetheless, this approach has been successfully applied to software development projects and is particularly useful when the initial requirements are either not very clear, when new technologies are being deployed, or when it is likely that customer requirements will change through the course of the project.

The PSC model

This model takes another, equally valid, approach to modelling the development process by accepting that several viewpoints or perspectives are considered. The main perspectives described within PSC are:

- *Pragmatic.* Views the system in the context of the existing environment.

- *Input/output.* Studies the external behaviour of the system and how it is to be achieved.

- *Constructive.* Examines the system in terms of a collection of functions and resources.

- *Operative.* Studies the internal behaviour of the system.

The use of PSC involves (as for the spiral) four main phases. This time each of the phases is concerned with the decision problems of one of the above perspectives. The model identifies the pragmatic as the most abstract level. In this phase the system is studied in terms of its relation with and impact on the environment in which it is to be placed. The model requires the design, test and assessment to be completed at this abstract level before moving on to the next phase.

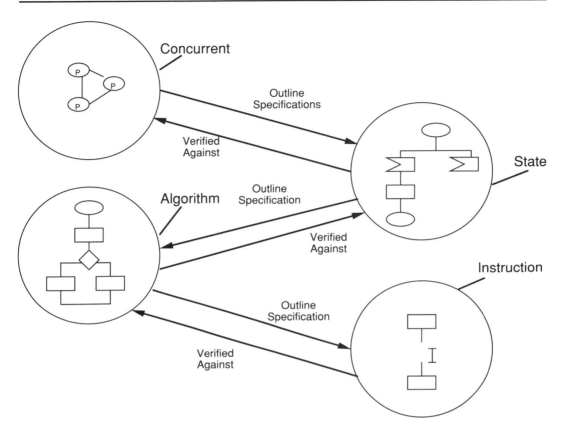

Figure 3.5   The structure levels of a typical telecomm systems

Adapted lifecycles

All of the examples given so far can be applied to any application area. To show how a particular lifecycle can be adapted for a particular purpose, we briefly illustrate it by showing what the system design part of the water- fall model might look like for the design of telecommunications software.

To start with, four distinct structural levels within the design activity, each with its own characteristics, have to be recognised, as illustrated in Figure 3.5. The nature of each of these structural levels can be explained as follows.

- At the *concurrent level* the system is viewed as a set of sequential pro- cesses which communicate. Each process is autonomous and interacts with other processes and with the environment to produce the required system behaviour.

- At the *sequential level* each of the processes in the system can be described as a finite-state machine which determines the actions to be performed, either from internal events or from messages received from the other processes in the system.

- At the *algorithm level* the individual actions or programs that comprise each process can be characterised as transformers of an input data structure into an output data structure.

- At the *instruction level* the basic primitives of the individual programs are described in terms of individual data elements and operations on data elements.

Since each of the above levels describes the components of the next higher level, the system is the sum of all levels. From a modelling viewpoint, the levels identified here are qualitatively different, each poses its own problems for the engineer and involves its own set of design decisions.

The next stage, therefore, is to find a precise and unambiguous way of capturing the concerns at each of the structural levels identified. This choice often depends on a number of diverse technical and operational factors [Jac86]. The important point is that this choice is explicit rather than a default. In the above example, the SDL design method (outlined in Chapter 5) formed the basis for support.

3.3   THE SOFTWARE DEATHCYCLE

Before moving away from the various lifecycle models it is worth noting one common feature in all of them: they concentrate on pre-delivery development. On the face of it this poses no problems since all design (whether it is pre- or post-delivery) is, in essence, the same. In practice, however, there *is* a problem with this simplification in that post-delivery design, in the form of enhancement, is usually coalesced (sometimes intentionally) with error correction. These activities are, however, qualitatively different and need to be separated from each other so that objective measurements of an increasingly important factor—cost—can be made.

A model that does address the problem is the 'software *deathcycle*' which contrasts with the conventional 'software lifecycle' in that the focus is on the cost of keeping a system rather than the economics of developing a new one [RN90] . This model is included here by way of illustration as its practical application is, to date, limited.

The basic premise that underlies the deathcycle model is that maintenance of a released system (to a given standard of quality) costs money and has to be offset against the benefits that accrue from that software. At some point, the cost of ownership begins to outweigh the benefit and this is the point at which net income goes negative. This is the point at which the software should be retired from use. The deathcycle is illustrated in Figure 3.6.

An immediate observation from Figure 3.6 is that the income during the development phase is nil. This phase just costs money. Exactly how much money is expended in this is subject to a great number of factors and will not be discussed here.

Once released, or put into operation, the software starts to earn. These earnings must account for a number of things, the most obvious of which is the ongoing cost of maintenance. It would clearly make no sense to develop a system that cost more to service than it was capable of earning. As stated earlier, the actual cost of maintaining software varies with, among other things, the required level of quality. Given this, the likely cost of keeping a known number of variants of a piece of software installed at a known number of locations could, to a reasonable first approximation, be estimated.

There are other factors over and above the maintenance costs that impinge on economic viability: the initial cost of development needs to be recouped over some period and, looking forward, there is a need to earn enough money to fund a replacement for the software when it eventually dies.

Looking to the right-hand side of Figure 3.6 there inevitably comes a time when income starts to decline and/or the amount of maintenance effort required to keep an acceptable level of quality becomes prohibitively expensive. If the expenditure on the software is more than the 'income' it generates, then it is time for it to be retired.

This simple graph can be used to model the impact of many of the planning decisions often made in isolation during a software project. Once the model is installed with appropriate forecasts, facts and figures, it enables software death to be explicitly acknowledged and planned. Examples of these planning decisions can be cited.

- *When design costs exceed the income forecast.* In some cases this may be acceptable, for instance if the strategic value of the software is paramount. Otherwise, some radical action is required. Either the cashflow forecasts have to be revised (e.g. the planned maintenance outlay may have to be cut) or the entire venture should be stopped.

- *When development time misses market window.* Explicit analysis of the whole life of the software shows both timing and volume of the product release. The estimated impact of missing expected market windows can readily be added to the analysis by way of adjustment.

- *When to replace.* Once the model is installed with the necessary figures, this decision becomes one of policy. For instance, preserving software through to its technical death (termination) may be required in some

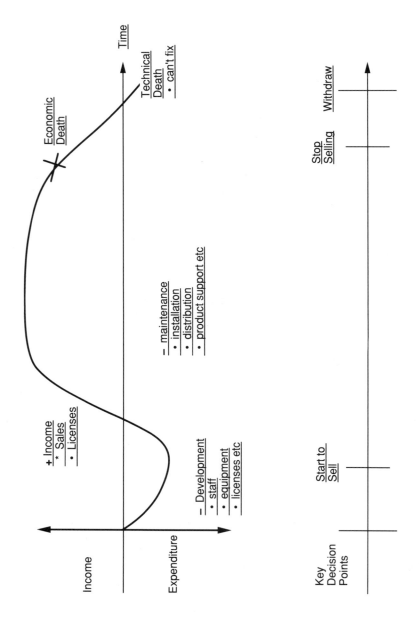

Figure 3.6 The software deathcycle

circumstances. It is clear from Figure 3.6 that the cost of doing this depends on the time between termination and economic death and by the required quality level.

One further important consequence of modelling the cost of software ownership across its lifetime is that it becomes possible to depreciate the software in the same way as other assets. This is an effective means of putting aside money to pay for a replacement—something that is rarely planned for in most accountancy schemes.

3.4   QUALITY IN THE LIFECYCLE

In any lifecycle model there are a number of issues that always have to be attended to [NCC87]. This section provides a brief checklist of some of the key issues that have to be performed if any sort of quality objectives are to be met.

Configuration management

This is the essential quality activity of keeping control of the issue and status of all hardware, documents, firmware and software. Failure to effect accurate configuration management can result in the loss of key components or in the integration of inappropriate ones. Control of changes is particularly important for software development since there is no visibility to the software stored on discs or of the content of PROMs other than via their labelling and documentation.

Documentation standards:

Since the only visible form of software is the documentation, a formal structure linking together specification, design documents (e.g. diagrams) and code listings is essential. Naturally these should be appropriate to the size of the software package. A few pages of requirements and flowcharts may well suffice for a small calculation package, whereas several volumes would be necessary to describe a large real-time process control or communications system.

Design standards

The need for an appropriate set of design representations was discussed in Chapter 2. In many ways the quality of a design depends on the skill, expe-

rience and intuition of the designer. Design methods do not supplant this—
they provide a systematic way of recording information so that it can be
validated, verified and kept for future reference. As systems grow more
complex and design teams grow larger, so the value of a common approach
to making and recording design decisions increases.

Metrics

The only way to improve quality is to establish what the current level is and
devise a plan for improvement. There are a number of important aspects
of software that can be measured. In terms of the software itself (product
measures), there are size metrics, complexity metrics, information flow
metrics, and many more. Equally important are measures of the process by
which the software is produced, such as time to fix a fault, etc.

As there are no established absolute values for software or its production,
it is vital to establish a relevant set of measures. Once these are established,
it is the correlations between individual measures that provide information
from the collected data. For instance, measurement might reveal that fault
reports rise exponentially with module complexity. This sort of information is invaluable in planning and controlling software projects.

Programming standards

Given an ultimate objective to write clear structured software using well-
defined modules with functions that are easily understood, there is no prize
for complexity. There are various methods for developing structure, including data flow, hierarchical and structured diagrams as well as pseudo code
(a form of high-level code using English language statements).

Design reviews

These are assessments of the design against the requirements [Fag76]. Since
the early design reviews are carried out before the product is ready for
demonstration or test they take the form of an assessment of the functions
provided by the design specifications. The aim of the design review is to
check conformance to common-sense standards and to higher levels of
design or requirements.

Code inspection and walkthrough (discussed in Chapter 6) are a part of
the later reviews and involve detailed examination of the code in order to
assess its capability of carrying out the requirements and its conformance
to standards.

Verification, validation and test

Testing, in the broadest sense of ensuring fitness for purpose, involves a number of methods. These are described in detail in Chapter 6. It is important to plan a structured set of tests which build on each other so that a predetermined level of confidence in designs and their subsequent implementation modules is reached before testing of subsystems (groups of modules) and, in turn, the entire system is integrated and ready for functional and environmental test. Types of test include: formal proof of correctness, validation of design by inspection or walkthrough, static tests, dynamic tests involving test data, etc.

Failure feedback

The more structured and formal the system of failure feedback, the faster and more reliable will be the achievement of required levels of quality. There are three distinct areas of failure data collection:

- Failure reporting prior to an item becoming subject to configuration control (e.g. during design).

- Failure reporting of a controlled module that has not been released.

- Field failure reporting from the user (including received requests for change).

Formal arrangements are required for each of the above, ranging from something as simple as a logbook in which a team of designers record test results to a product support unit which formally records user problems and change requests.

All of the above are essential quality activities that involve setting standards and auditing progress against the stated requirements [IDP86]. Although this provides an environment for reducing the likelihood of errors, it does not impact on the fundamental reasons for their existence; this is why we need now to examine not the process of producing quality systems but also the techniques which help at each stage in production.

Good techniques of design, testing, requirements capture, etc. seek to replace error-prone activities with more formal or structured approaches that minimise error and maximise the chances of creating a reliable product [Mul85]. One of the primary objectives of this book is to outline a range of techniques that have proved effective in practice. The remainder of the book is concerned with explaining appropriate techniques across the whole of the software lifecycle. In addition to this, attention is paid to some of the evolving techniques, tools and attitudes which need to dominate software design if its reliability is to equal or exceed the associated hardware.

3.5   THE PRACTICALITIES OF USING LIFECYCLE MODELS

Many designers ignore all of the above approaches and proceed with coding when only a part of the total design is conceived. Short-term commercial pressures often make this almost unavoidable.

Some design teams succeed in applying the techniques outlined in a realistic and conscientious way. The result is much higher quality software than would otherwise have been the case and, more important, the errors in both design and code are discovered and rectified at the earliest opportunity.

A very small number of organisations have invested in the design and programming tools which automate quality techniques and help to prevent software faults by highlighting inconsistencies as they occur. These tools vary from Computer Aided Software Engineering (CASE) tools which typically concentrate on one aspect of software development, right through to full 'environments' of tools which provide facilities for design capture and expression, code production, context- and syntax-sensitive editors, test aids and configuration management. These tools (often referred to as Integrated Project Support Environments, IPSEs) are just beginning to emerge and are likely to have a strong impact on software development in large systems.

One of the essential precursors to introducing IPSE facilities is to have a clear idea of what development process is appropriate. Much of what is described in this chapter will therefore have to be adopted at some point in any software development organisation that wishes to capitalise on the next generation of support tools.

3.6   SUMMARY

The simple message in this chapter is that it is important to understand the software development process. We have tried to show how software lifecycle models can be used to provide a 'map' of what is going on amid the welter of diagrams, documents and magic formulae that inevitably accompany all software developments. The point is made that no lifecycle model is either perfect or generic. There are good reasons for this:

- All lifecycle models are idealised abstractions. They do not aim to model the precise details and imperfections of the real world.

- Different lifecycles take different views. This is primarily a reflection of the different approaches to development. The conventional sequential staged development is well served by the waterfall model and its many variations and refinements. The snail or PSC models are well suited to projects based around prototyping techniques.

- They are not application specific. Some work is still required to install actual languages, tools, etc. to suit a particular task. This is, however, a fairly straightforward exercise, as outlined in the example given here.

- They are usually focused on the technical aspects of development. Links to other parameters, such as costs, have to be built on. Even so the existing lifecycles do provide a sound basis: the cost model outlined in this chapter (the software *deathcycle*) was built up from an established lifecycle model.

Given these limitations, the adoption of appropriate lifecycle models is an important step towards improving quality. It is the first move in bringing the software development process under control. Once this is achieved the way is open to study, refine and automate that process.

3.7   REFERENCES

[Ago88] Agostoni, G. *et al* (1988) Managing software quality during the complete lifecycle *1st European Seminar on Software Quality* (Brussels, 1988).

[Fag76] Fagan, M. (1976) 'Design and code inspections to reduce errors in program development' *IBM Systems Journal* **15.4**.

[IDP86] Institute of Data Processing Managers (1986) *The Grindley Report.*

[Jac86] Jackson, L.A. (1986) Software system design methods and the engineering approach *BT Technical Journal* **14.3**.

[KF81] Kerola, P. and Freeman, P. (1981) A comparison of life cycle model *Proc. 5th Int. Conf. on Software Engineering* (San Diego, 1981).

[Mul85] Mullery, G. (1985) 'Acquisition-environment, in *Distributed Systems: Methods and Tools for Specification'* (*Lecture Notes in Computer Science 190*) ed. M. Paul and H. Siegert (Springer-Verlag).

[NCC87] National Computer Centre/DTI (1987) *The STARTS Guide. A Guide to Software Methods and Tools* pp 44–59.

[RN90] Rigby, P. and Norris, M. The software death cycle *Proc. UK IT 90 Conference* (March 1990).

4
System Requirements

We know what we are but we know not what we may become
William Shakespeare (Hamlet)

One of the points illustrated in previous chapters is that many software projects fail not because they do not work but simply because they do the wrong thing. The capture and analysis of system requirements is one of the most important phases in a successful project, yet the time and effort devoted to this activity is usually minimal.

In this chapter we move on from the general and begin to explore a specific part of the process of software development—requirements. The structure of this and the next three chapters (which also concentrate on a particular part of the lifecycle) is similar. First the subject matter is explained—in this case we outline the scope of requirements capture and analysis and describe some of the basic principles and ideas. Then we look at some of the known problems that arise in this phase and give a brief introduction to some of the tools and techniques that have been used. Much of this section is primarily for illustration as the tools and techniques used in practice change and evolve rapidly. Finally, we provide a checklist against which key requirements issues may be assessed.

4.1 SCOPE OF REQUIREMENTS

All of the software development lifecycles described earlier include a phase for explicit agreement to be reached on the responsibilities of both purchaser and supplier during contract execution—the *Requirements specification*. The exact role of the requirements specification in the development process depends upon the particular lifecycle employed. However, the requirements specification always fulfils the following two roles:

- It provides the primary input to the design phase.

- It gives a baseline against which acceptance tests are carried out.

Before looking at what is involved in the requirements process, it is worth dwelling on its aim.

It is widely accepted that the cost of correcting/modifying a system after installation or indeed after the early stages of the design phase are high and likely to be greater than the cost of preparing an adequate requirements specification in the first place. As a rule of thumb, the cost of repairing an error rises by a factor of ten from one phase of development to the next [Boe81], as shown in Figure 4.1.

Thus the preparation of an adequate requirements specification both reduces cost and reduces overall risk attached to the development.

A clear definition of what should be included in the requirements specification is not straightforward. The distinction between requirements and design has always been easy to state and hard to clarify:

- *Requirement.* What the system must do.

- *Design.* How the system should do it.

These definitions are somewhat arbitrary and need to be further refined as it is difficult to make a clear distinction between clarification of requirements and high-level design. An ideal requirements specification should say what the purchaser requires (in terms of the system and its environment), e.g. relating inputs to outputs. It says nothing about the structure of the system but should state constraints (e.g. time to delivery).

Unfortunately structure is often a key to understanding. Unstructured requirements specifications are often obscure and defeat their intended purpose. In practice a compromise has to be made and some structure is placed on the system, i.e function decomposition, data/activity. The right balance is a matter of personal opinion, experience and debate.

To clarify the arbitrary distinction between design and requirements we will use Figure 4.2 [Coh87] to model the interaction between customer and supplier.

On its own the diagram is of little help. However, it does clarify one important distinction that needs to be drawn—that there are two main deliverables from the activity referred to as requirements capture and analysis.

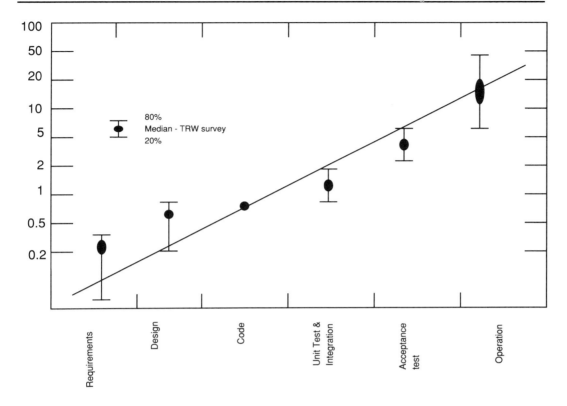

Figure 4.1   The increasing costs of fixing errors through its life of software

These can be identified with two phases of the process as follows:

- *Phase 1:*
  — To elicit background information and understand the role the system is expected to play in the environment. Usually followed by a more detailed description of the requirements from the user's viewpoint.
  — The informal basis of agreeing what is to be done.

- *Phase 2:*
  — A fully detailed specification of the requirements.
  — The formal statement of what is to be delivered.

The options for realising phase 2 as defined above are covered in some detail in the next chapter. For the remainder of this chapter we will concentrate on the altogether more nebulous topic of extracting a clear idea of what it is that the user wants.

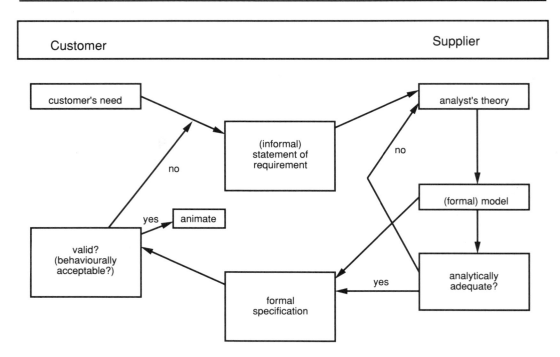

Figure 4.2   The split between requirements and design

4.2   BASIC PRINCIPLES AND IDEAS

There are several distinct approaches to generating requirements, depending on the development lifecycle being used. Each approach implies different needs in terms of the type of information being captured, the level of risk in its application and the most appropriate method used for collection. The two most common approaches are:

- *Contractual.* A full requirements specification will be developed prior to system development. This is a most appropriate strategy when, for instance, the waterfall model of development is used.

- *Evolutionary.* A partial requirements specification (for the core system) will be developed prior to initial development, full functionality requiring subsequent analysis during the development. The spiral model of development applies in this case.

The choice is either dictated by the purchaser, or chosen by the supplier, depending on the type of scenario which the development is expected to follow. The most common scenarios are:

- Replacement of the existing system with little or no modification.

- The integration of two or more existing systems.

- A completely new system with known, identifiable, tangible users.

- A completely new system with no readily identifiable users.

The last two scenarios would be well suited to the evolutionary strategy, the others to the contractual strategy. In general, the expected scenario is often a good guide to the kind of information that the requirements analysis phase seeks to clarify.

The requirements capture and analysis phase of a development typically concentrates on the following information:

- The business process to be supported and business benefit to be realised.

- The user community—who the users will be and how they will interact with the system.

- Market analysis—what the impact of the system will be: how much it will cost and how much it will earn/save.

- Existing system and its documentation.

- Priority of requirements.

The appropriate choice of *Requirements analysis method* depends on the overall approach which should be related to the *scenario*, which in turn influences the balance of the Information that is required.

Ideally the responsibility for the production of the requirements specification should be that of the purchaser's organisation with the supplier only being required to comment/correct/question on engineering and feasibility grounds. However, it is often the case that the purchaser's organisation does not possess the necessary skills to define the full requirement. More typically, it is the job of the supplier to ensure that a consistent and realistic set of requirements are gathered. In doing this there are a number of important and distinct information classes that need to be recognised. The three key input classes are:

- Initial input from the user(s).

- Change requests arising from changes in the system environment, or perception of the environment.

- Change requests arising from the development process and system use.

The balance of the above input classes depends on the approach chosen and the stage reached in the project. Overall, the process of requirements capture and analysis must deal with:

- gathering information

- producing agreed terminology

- verification of internal consistency and completeness

- ensuring that the requirements specification reflects the capabilities of technology

- making a clear distinction between requirements and design

- identifying the system boundaries

- encompassing all relevant views

- enabling controlled changes to be introduced

- noting all relevant constraints imposed (e.g. computing platform)

- ensuring that the external quality requirements (performance, etc.) are explicitly recorded.

The above serves as a checklist against some of the recognised requirements analysis methods described and explained later on in this chapter.

4.3 THE MAIN PROBLEM AREAS

The preparation of a requirements specification is difficult. It must describe every possible aspect of system behaviour, thus requiring a complete understanding of the purchaser's problems, desires and environment in which the system will eventually be installed. Thus the scope of the requirements specification makes its production a specialist task which is made more difficult by a number of factors including:

- The tendency for information, which is thought to be 'obvious' to the purchaser, to be omitted.

- Purchasers and suppliers often use different terminology leading to a communications problem, which is often only recognised in the design phase or later, where correction/modification is expensive.

- Purchasers are often uncertain about the capabilities and limitations of current technology (subject to 'hype') and can often state unreasonable requirements.

- The definition of the system boundary, i.e. what functionality is performed within the system and what is performed without, is often not clear.

- Different users often have incompatible requirements or views of the system and reconciliation is necessary.

- Requirements are always subject to change due to changes in the environment and in understanding of both customer and supplier as the development progresses.

- The testing of requirements is often impossible, e.g. 'The system must be user friendly'.

- Compromise due to economic, engineering and acceptability factors is often made.

- The distinction between requirements and design is often blurred.

These factors , and others, make it very important that a good method with tool support is available to support the requirements capture stage process. Although rather dated, Figure 4.3 highlights the problem being tackled in the requirements phase. It shows the fate of a group of US DoD software projects—only 1.5% of which were delivered and used with no modification. The largest proportion of non-compliant systems were completed but not used. The main lesson from this was that it is vital to know what the customer really wants.

4.4 CURRENT APPROACHES TO REQUIREMENTS CAPTURE AND ANALYSIS

There are many techniques available [Dar90] for requirements capture and analysis (resulting in the construction of a requirements specification). These fall into one of three broad categories:

- *Standards.* A definition of the content and approval criteria of a requirements specification.

- *Methods.* A set of rules for the aquisition, analysis and testing (checking) of required information.

- *Tools.* Automated aids generally supporting the control of the volume of information, checks to ensure consistency and checks for completeness.

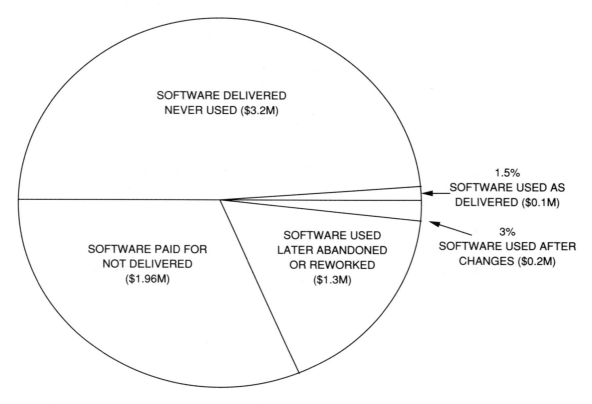

Figure 4.3   Usability of software contracted by US DoD

Standards

A few standards exist and all agree that an ideal requirements specification would have the following characteristics:

- *Unambiguous.* Every requirement should have only one interpretation. A glossary of terms can help but natural language has pitfalls and to overcome this, formal and semi-formal languages can be used where applicable.

- *Complete.* All significant requirements and aspects of the environment, whether relating to functionality, performance, design constraints, etc., should be included.

- *Verifiable.* In the sense that the requirement must be stated in such a way that the system can be tested to ensure that the requirement has been fulfilled.

- *Consistent.* There should be no conflict between individual requirements.

- *Modifiable.* Users alter their requirement on an almost continuous basis and the requirements specification should therefore be organised in such a way as to accommodate this (i.e. well structured and cross-referenced).

- *Traceable.* Reference mechanisms are needed to allow backward and forward traceability.

- *Useable during operational and maintenance phases.* Attention needs to be paid to operational and maintenance needs and the updating of requirements specifications to meet these needs, especially where failure of a component could be critical or where temporary changes are made.

- *Intelligible.* Requirements have to be read and understood by many people—users, analysts, purchasers and suppliers. The requirements specification forms the basis for communication between all the different classes of people involved in a development.

Some of the better known standards are the European Space Agency Software Engineering Standard PSS-05-0 Issue 1 (1987) and the IEEE 830 standard. The requirements section of these standards defines an overall scope and structure of a user's requirements document and defines criteria for its assessment. In the UK, the STARTS purchasers' guide provides a great deal of useful information.

Methods

Widely recognised requirements capture and analysis methods are few in number although many development methods do acknowledge the importance of this process and attempt to provide guidelines to aid it. Typically requirements methods fall into the following three categories—informal, semi-formal and formal.

Informal (notations with no fixed syntax or semantics)

The notation used is usually natural language, supported by *ad hoc* diagrams with no formal, predefined meaning. These approaches rarely have any defined procedures for requirements capture, verification or validation. However, they are easy to apply, require little training and assist with understanding of the system. This can be something of an illusion, however, as they are only as good as the people who use them. An example of an informal method would be Checkland's soft system method.

Semi-formal (structured)

These methods typically employ graphical notations (diagrams) with well defined syntax and reasonably well defined semantics (often supported by natural language). They also have a well defined set of procedures and guidelines. These approaches offer greater scope for achieving consistency, completeness and clarity and are often good vehicles for communication; however, the expressive power of the notation tends to be limited and these methods tend to view the world in a very simple way. Specification methods such as SSADM, Information Engineering and CORE fall into this category.

Formal

These approaches employ a precise mathematical notation which can be highly expressive; however, they tend to high training requirements even to facilitate their reading (this can actually hinder rather than help user/developer communication) and are narrow in focus. The training costs for their developers are even higher. FOREST is an example of a formal method for requirements.

Most methods are primarily concerned with the production of the requirements specification document and do not address the process of requirements capture in any detail, often only supplying simple guidelines on interview techniques and sometimes key areas which should be investigated but are often forgotten (e.g. security, training etc.).

Almost all requirements capture and analysis methods use a process-oriented approach, or a representation-oriented approach (or both) in order to express the requirements and provide a framework for analysis. Unfortunately both of these traditional views of a system tend towards the implementation view of system engineering.

Representation-oriented approaches are typified by the *Entity Relationship Attribute* (ERA) model which permits the description of systems in terms of entities (objects) of various types, the interrelationships among these entities and their specific properties or attributes. Standards are then applied to the ERA model to determine the relevant object types, relationships and properties together with corresponding consistency and completeness tests.

Process-oriented approaches are typified by the *Data Flow Diagram* (DFD) which describes a system as a network of processes connected to each other by paths over which data can flow (these diagrams are further explained in the next chapter). The basic components of these networks are process, data flows and stores. Data flow diagrams are hierarchical; each process can be expanded and detailed by several more processes. A set of standards are applied to the DFD to check for consistency.

Some methods employ both approaches (e.g structured analysis) in which case the system is modelled using both complementary models independently and then cross-referenced for consistency checking. Such methods often assume that no individual can completely understand the whole system and provide techniques for controlled teamwork.

CORE method

Perhaps the most widely used method that focuses on requirements analysis is CORE. Given that this method has been widely used since its appearance in1979, and is one of the more mature available, we outline its main features below.

The COntrolled Requirements Expression (CORE) method is a set of textual and graphical notations, with specified guidelines for the capture and validation of system requirements, at the initial stages of system design. CORE has been traditionally thought of purely as a requirements capture and analysis (RCA) technique, although it does support some aspects of design, such as data structuring. CORE is based on the principle of first defining the problem to be analysed (*problem definition*), then breaking it down into units or *viewpoints* to be considered. As the analysis progresses, these viewpoints and the relationships between them become more distinct.

The CORE method consists of seven stages. Each stage produces outputs that either feed into subsequent stages as input or that form part of the final requirements specification. CORE attempts to examine the system and its environment at a number of levels, with progressively finer detail at each level. The seven stages are summarised below:

1. *Problem definition.* The purpose of problem definition is to identify problem boundaries. The output of this stage is a *problem statement* document, which should not be of more than two or three pages. It contains details of the business objectives of the system's users, the basis for needing a new system, cost and time limitations and who is going to be responsible for reviewing and accepting the final results. The general aim of this stage is to achieve a consensus on the general problem.

2. *Viewpoint structuring.* The aim of this stage is to decompose the environment of the system down into its components so that the proposed system can be analysed from the viewpoints of all the entities that communicate with it, the most important of which are the users. Thus during this stage, all the entities which are potential sources or sinks of information should be identified.

3. *Tabular collection.* This stage is when information about data flows between viewpoints and the processing at viewpoints is gathered. This aids establishing completeness and consistency. At each successive viewpoint level, more detail is introduced. This stage produces *Tabular Collection Forms* (TCF).

4. *Data structuring.* In the previous stage, the items of information passing between viewpoints are referred to by general names. In this stage, a closer look is taken at the content, structure and derivation of the data, by producing *data structure diagrams.*

5. *Single viewpoint modelling.* This stage can be split into two parts. The sole concern of the first part is with converting the TCF's into a different notation to produce the *single viewpoint model diagrams.* The second part is concerned with adding some new information pertaining to internal data flows, control of actions, and timing of actions.

6. *Combined viewpoint modelling.* This stage facilitates analysis of a sequence of events from more than one viewpoint. Each *combined viewpoint model diagram* produced during this stage is a representation of the information processing that occurs between viewpoints.

7. *Constraints analysis.* At this stage, additional constraints such as performance and reliability are considered. These may affect the viewpoint diagrams already produced. The constraints are documented in a *system constraints specification.*

- *Application areas.* The major applications of CORE have been in the real-time domain, particularly in the avionics industry, mainly due to the methods source, British Aerospace. The size of projects that CORE has been used on varies from small (1–2 man-years), to very large (more than 500 man-years). Known users of CORE now include the systems designers, the Ministry of Defence, Plessey and British Telecom. In essence, CORE provides no more than codified commonsense. Other methods, such as Information Engineering, cover similar ground and are becoming more widely used, primarily because of available support tools (IEF).

Tools

Most support tools employ a *Requirements Specification Language* (RSL). An RSL is the means for communicating information between the purchaser (or user) to a tool and from the tool to the purchaser. An RSL needs to be:

1. Sufficiently precise to allow a set of specification statements to be checked for consistency and completeness.

2. Natural enough to permit human comprehension.

Clearly, the above two desirable characteristics conflict (i.e. mathematical notations satisfy 1, but at the expense of 2). In practice a compromise is likely. The precision required for automated tool support means that an RSL must be based on some formal system model which is naturally human comprehensible.

RSLs fall into two main categories:

- Fixed terminology languages.

- Definable terminology languages.

Few have directly associated methods, and none provide a perfect solution, but they have been applied successfully to assist the production of better-quality requirements specifications than those achieved by purely manual means.

Computer-based tools which provide automated assistance in the production and maintenance of requirements specifications by using an RSL share the following basic characteristics:

- A system description database which holds the current (not necessarily complete) set of specifications in a fully cross-referenced form.

- Facilities to manipulate the contents of the database (input, etc.) with checks.

- Analysis methods to check consistency and completeness.

- Presentation facilities to allow extraction and presentation of information held in the database according to predefined, or *ad hoc* user-supplied criteria.

A typical tool for requirements capture and analysis is the *Problem Statement Language, Problem Statement Analyser* (PSL/PSA) system. The problem statement language is a relational, non-procedural and machine-processable language with well defined syntax and semantics, and is designed for systems description. The underlying system model is the entity relationship attribute (ERA) model describing objects, their properties and binary relations between these objects. System descriptions are classified as:

- System input/output flows.

- Data structure.

- Data derivation.

- System size and volume.

- System dynamics.

- System properties and project management.

The problem statement analyser is a collection of computer software developed for the processing and analysis of PSL statements, and the management of the database information. Lexical, syntactic and semantic analysis is performed on the PSL statements before they are entered into the database. PSA is able to perform the following:

- Static analysis (to check consistency of input statements).

- Dynamic analysis (to determine dynamic relationships among input, output, and timing consistency of processes).

- Volume analysis.

PSL/PSA was not originally developed to fit any particular system development framework but has been successfully incorporated into several, for instance, SAFRA—the method developed by British Aerospace combining elements of CORE, PSL/PSA and MASCOT. As with methods, tools in this area change rapidly and should be chosen to suit local needs.

4.5   A GENERAL APPROACH

So far this chapter has looked at the problems of gathering accurate requirements and has outlined some of the current approaches being used. Since there is no agreed way of tackling requirements analysis, a simple model is explained below as an example for tackling this important first part of the development process.

Ideally, three definitions are required to ensure that the system requirements are thoroughly analysed:

1. A specification of the *current* situation, in which problems (and opportunities for improvement) reside.

2. A specification of the *target* situation, including a stated set of goals (usually encompassing some or all of the identified problems).

3. A specification of how the current situation can be transformed into the target situation.

In the approach explained here, it is intended that the three definitions should largely be produced in the order listed. This is a controversial
point. Most analysis techniques tend to be goal-driven (see e.g. [Mul79]),
encouraging the analyst to 'develop positive statements' rather than
dwell on current problems. Also, strategic goals are often defined by
the client before analysis starts. Nevertheless, in some cases it is beneficial to gain a full understanding of the current situation before moving
on to consider how improvements can be made. The main reasons for
this are:

● It is usually necessary to have some knowledge of the current situation
before considering the target situation whereas the current situation can
be explored in isolation.

● It is easier to set (or analyse) goals in the context of the current system.

A common idea in trying to understand and rationalise requirements is to
break a large, complex problem into its constituent parts, cross-referencing
the parts one with another and explaining all of the links that are established. In effect this builds a cognitive map [Tol48] of the set of goals which
provides a model that can be systematically analysed and kept for future
reference.

Application of the basic approach is considered below in two different
areas of application—one concerned with ensuring that a situation is analysed adequately, the other with assisting the objective review of textual
descriptions.

Types of analysis

Any complex system requires many opinions and considerations to be taken
into account. The technique described here requires analysis against a number of criteria [Bus90]. The scope of this analysis with respect to stated (e.g.
given through interview, etc) requirements is summarised below:

Relevance analysis

Here a table is constructed of the requirements and those whom they affect.
An attempt is made to assess the relevance of each requirement to each
individual (or group) involved. The requirements can then be prioritised
according to their total assessed relevance. Those affected can, similarly, be
put into a priority order according to the number and extent of the requirements that affect them.

Quality analysis

Any set of requirements can be examined with respect to a basic set of quality attributes, as introduced in Chapter 1. The extent to which identified requirements impinge on these attributes should then be examined. Once again a table can be used, and through it the most significant requirements become evident as do those attributes that are most affected.

Interaction analysis

Requirements are rarely independent, so attempting to meet any one will tend to contribute to the achievement of one or more others. In some cases, fulfilling one requirement may have a detrimental effect on others. Once again a table can be used to clarify the interrelationships that are present and estimates made of the dependencies involved. This gives a means of identifying requirements that can be pursued in isolation and grouping those that need to be treated collectively.

An example of how the *relevance analysis* is applied is shown in Figure 4.4. It shows the extent to which each of a system's stated requirements (numbered from 1 to 7) impact the known users. The requirements are numbered across the top of the table and roles are identified down the left-hand side. Cells in the grid hold values on an arbitrary scale of −9 to +9. A value of zero represents a neutral position. A positive value indicates that a particular goal is of concern to a particular actor (e.g. influences what they do, how they do it, etc.). A negative value indicates that an actor believes that an attempt to satisfy the goal is undesirable. On the right-hand side, the absolute values in each row have been summed to identify those who have expressed the strongest feelings. At the bottom of the table the columns have been summed to show the combined feelings of the actors about each goal. These values serve as an aid to comparing goals and putting them into a priority order. Note, however, that the sums only provide a rough guide for the analyst. They should not and, indeed, cannot be used as the sole basis for decision taking. The difficulties to appreciate are:

1. In general, summed values in a decision table cannot be used to identify a priority order unless the entities being compared are independent.

2. The summations assume that all goals and all actors are equally important. This is not true of goals and probably less true of actors.

3. The values are based on ordinal, not interval, scaling. The summations should therefore be regarded as indications only.

Goal Number									
	1	2	3	4	5	6	7		$|\Sigma|$
Directors	8	8	2	2	3	4	0		27
Managers	-2	1	8	-4	9	9	5		26
Customers	9	3	2	7	-1	-2	9		27
Σ	15	12	12	5	11	11	14		

Role (label for rows)

Figure 4.4 Relevance analysis

Despite these limitations, the values capture the perception of the users and serve as a basis for discussion on how the target situation might be defined. In practice, each value in the table needs to be supported with explanatory text so that the rationale behind the scores is not lost. The preparation of this type of table serves two useful purposes. First, it enables inconsistencies and anomalies to be highlighted and, second, it provides a record of requirements analysis that serves for future reference.

Validation

Even after requirements are clearly understood, they still have to be written down and (usually) refined. At any point in writing down a description of a system, the text has to be very clear. Natural language, the main medium for such descriptions, is notorious for its vagueness and openness to misinterpretation. In general, graphical descriptions are little better in that they often rely on the user's perception for their meaning; the basic problem is one of semantics, not syntax. Given the fairly specialised set of applications that draw full benefit from formal, mathematical system descriptions, there is a need to make natural language text as easy to understand and interpret as possible.

The requirements for comprehending a specification (or proposed solution) are somewhat different from those for clarifying the relationship among a set of goals. Internal consistency and completeness are the main concerns for the former. The latter is more an exercise in the collation of ideas and opinions. Nonetheless, a similar approach is effective in both cases: that of breaking the whole down into parts and identifying/explaining relations among them.

To be more specific, the technique described in this Section is a simple extension of ideas developed for code analysis into documentation by requiring extra documentation to be generated which enables more rigorous review. The purpose of this extra documentation is to ensure that ideas and concepts introduced in a description are clearly identified and explained.

In operation, this technique calls for a description to be generated in two separate but related parts. The first part is a *narrative* document which is given in a tutorial style and which, of necessity, will contain various words and phrases that have precise or particular meanings within the document. The second part is the *reference* which provides a definition for all of the keywords and phrases in the narrative part. Keywords introduced or used in the reference document must themselves be defined so that possible errors can be traced through.

Together, the narrative and reference documents constitute a reviewable specification set. The impact of providing detailed descriptions of terms used is that reviewers can readily check for consistency and, since keywords are identified in the reference as well as in the narrative, it is relatively easy to spot incomplete definitions.

A general consequence of the type of systematic analysis illustrated in this Section is that it ensures more issues than usual are considered and that all terms are defined. Although no objective evidence has yet been established to confirm (or deny) the effectiveness of this approach, similarly based techniques are routinely used for the review of software code and have proved effective. This effectiveness readily transfers to the analysis of requirements.

4.6   A REQUIREMENTS CHECKLIST

The previous section illustrated some of the ideas that can be used in generating a sound requirements specification. Given the nebulous nature of requirements it is all to easy, though, to miss important (sometimes essential) attributes that the system must possess. The only reliable way to minimise the occurance of such omissions is to ensure that experienced people gather and collate the system requirements. Given that this is not always possible, the next best thing is to use a checklist. A brief one concludes this chapter.

There are four key aspects of requirements capture and analysis in the checklist. Under each heading are the two or three key questions that need to be answered.

Information

- Does the information gathered include non-functional requirements— the important 'user quality attributes' introduced in Chapter 1 (security, performance, usability, reliability, etc.)?

- Have the views of all of those affected by the system and its development been included in the requirements gathering process?

- Have issues wider than the system functions and qualities been included (e.g. contractural obligations, technical constraints or cost and time limits)?

Analysis

- Is a mechanism in place to maintain (and if possible, check for consistency of) all of the information gathered?

- Are there criteria for prioritising requirements?

Accuracy

- Is the customer involved in and committed to reviewing the statement of requirements?

- Is the statement of requirements expressed in a suitable form (e.g. for a binding definition a formal specification may be required; a series of prototypes may suffice when the supplier and customer work closely together)?

- Are non-functional requirements either quantified (e.g. statements of performance, reliability) or expressed in a way that admits objective testing (e.g. usability in terms of time to learn)?

The requirements process

- Is it clear who the customer is?

- Is it clear why the system is required—are the objectives, terms of reference and expected deliverables from this phase known?

- Are the reasons for decision made recorded along with the decisions themselves and is the information gathered kept under some form of change control?

- If costing is part of the requirements phase, are issues such as training, maintenance, field support, installation, etc. considered?

The above list is by no means exhaustive but does cover most of the main concerns in the generation of a well structured and complete set of system requirements. In practice, requirements capture and analysis is often merged with the first stages of specification and design and it can be difficult to differentiate. Nonetheless the many questions posed above should be answered, at least to the satisfaction of whoever is responsible for delivering the system.

4.7 SUMMARY

The process of establishing the requirements of a software (or any other) system is an essential first step in delivering what the customer wants. Despite this, insufficient time and effort is often allocated for this activity and there are few systematic methods to support it. This chapter has defined what is involved in gathering requirements and outlined what the major problems encountered in practice are.

The approaches for tackling the requirements problem explained in this chapter fall into three categories:

- *Standards*. These define the content and approval criteria of a requirements Specification (e.g. the IEEE 803 standard).

- *Methods*. Rules and procedures for the acquisition and analysis of information, ranging from the informal through to the formal. The CORE method is outlined in the text as representative of this category.

- *Tools*. Automated aids that support the control of volumes of information, check for consistency and completeness. As an example PSA/PSL is explained in the main text.

Given the relative dearth of techniques to help with requirements capture (compared to, for instance, design) a large part of the chapter has been concerned with giving simple but practical guidelines. Some straightforward analytical techniques are illustrated which can be used to prioritise:

- *Relevance analysis*. Requirements and those whom they affect are cross-referenced in an attempt to assess the relevance of each requirement to each individual (or group) involved. This allows requirements to be prioritised according to their total assessed relevance. Those affected can, similarly, be put into a priority order according to the number and extent of the requirements that affect them.

- *Quality analysis*. Requirements are examined with respect to a basic set of quality attributes such as efficiency, reliability, and so on. The extent to which identified requirements impinge on these quality attributes can then be examined.

- *Interaction analysis.* In some cases, fulfilling one requirement may have a detrimental effect on others. This type of analysis gives a means of identifying requirements that can be pursued in isolation and grouping those that need to be treated collectively.

In addition to these techniques, a checklist covering the key aspects of the requirements phase is included at the end of the chapter to give some feel of what information should be included in the statement of requirements, how it should be assessed and how the overall requirements gathering process should be controlled.

There is little argument that the establishment of a clear and consistent set of requirements is an essential part of developing any software system. Likewise, there are few people who would claim that there exists a well established process to achieve this.

This chapter has outlined what is available in the way of techniques for the requirements phase and has illustrated some of the basic principles that can be put to good effect.

4.8 REFERENCES

[AY89] Arthur Young Ltd (1989) *Information Engineering Methodology.*

[Boe81] Boehm, B. (1981) *Software Engineering Economics* (Prentice Hall).

[Bus90] Bustard, D.W. , Norris, M.T. and Van Toen, B. (1990) Capturing and analysing user problems: separating the 'why' from the 'what', *Proc. Software Engineering '90 Conference* (Brighton).

[Coh87] Cohen, B. (1987) The education of the information systems engineer, *Electronics and Power* pp 203–205.

[Dar90] Davis, A.M. (1990) *Software Requirements, Analysis and Specification* (Prentice Hall).

[Ede89] Eden, C. (1989) Using cognitive mapping for strategic options development and analysis (SODA), in *Rational Analysis for a Problematic World*, ed. J. Rosenhead, (Wiley).

[KW86] Kitchenham, B.A. and Walker, J.G. (1986) The meaning of quality, *Proc. Software Engineering '86 Conference* (Southampton) (Peter Peregrinus).

[Mul79] Mullery, G. (1979) CORE—a method for controlled requirements specification, *Proc. 4th International Conference on Software Engineering.*

[Rom85] Roman, G.C. (1985) A taxonomy of current issues in requirements engineering, *Computer*, **18.4**, pp 14–21.

[Tol48] Tollman, E.C. (1948) Cognitive maps in rats and men, *Psychological Review*, **55**, pp 189–208.

5

Software Design

One cannot live in the shadow of an idea without grasping it
Elizabeth Bowden

The output from the requirements phase of any project, as described in the previous chapter, should be a statement of what the user wants. Assuming that this need is to be fulfilled by a software system, the next step is to turn the user statement of requirements into a computer-oriented specification of the requirement. The specification is then refined, developed and eventually implemented as a operational system that conforms to the original requirement. This is the process of software design.

Given that the transformation of any non-trivial set of requirements into a working system requires both precision and creativity, it is clear that software design is a demanding activity. The purpose of software design is to specify the internal structure and processing details of a system and to provide an audit trail of why design decisions were made. At present, there are few absolutes that can be applied to the software design process—good design relies, primarily, on talented and experienced designers. Nonetheless it is possible to supplement the skills of the software designer by adopting systematic software design methods and tools. This chapter aims to provide a view of the key issues in software design and the current design notations, method and tools that are available. As in the last chapter, a short checklist covering some of the key design issues is included at the end of the chapter.

5.1 SCOPE OF SOFTWARE DESIGN

As stated above, software design bridges the gap between the user's statement of requirements and the realisation of those requirements in the form of executable code. This definition covers a very broad range of activities and it is useful to break it down into two main areas—architectural design and detailed software design.

- *Architectural System Design.* This is the process during which a complete, verified specification of the overall hardware–software architecture, data structure, components and interfaces for the software product is produced. Along with this must go other necessary components such as draft user manuals and outline ('black box') test plans The requirement statement is elaborated with implementation-oriented specification detail during this phase.

- *Detailed Software Design.* This is when complete, verified specifications of the data structures, components and interfaces, sizing, key algorithms, and assumptions for each program component, leading on to programming, are produced. Again, supplementary information such as detailed test ('white box') specifications and documentation showing the structure of the implementation is required.

5.2   BASIC PRINCIPLES AND IDEAS

There are many different (and sometimes conflicting) factors that the designer has to take into account before deciding how to approach the design phase of a software development [Wal85]. Some of these are explained below along with the reasons why they need to be addressed The checklist at the end of the chapter refers back to this list.

- *Constraints.* There are a number of reasons why the full range of choices open to a designer would be restricted. Some of these are contractual (purchasers require certain procedures to be followed or methods to be used), others are technical (existing hardware and software limits the freedom to design from scratch).

- *Customer expectation.* The level of customer involvement in a software project may influence (and be influenced by) the design strategy adopted. If the design process is easy to monitor, the customer can contribute. This is not always desirable, nor is it always sought.

- *Type of system.* The nature of the system being developed does, to some extent, lead the choice of design methods and tools. For example, the most appropriate methods might be state tables for a real-time system such as OSI standard communication software, Oracle/SQL for a database design, object-oriented design for a distributed system, etc.

- *Type of application.* The implications of designing a security or safety critical system are very different (and make different demands on the design process) from the design of an in-house prototype.

- *Project environment*. There is little value in trying to introduce specific design practices into an organisation until it is equipped to capitalise on them. Factors such as the level of training and experience, and the support infrastructure (computing and organisational) come under this heading.

- *Whole lifecycle view.* Design choices should be taken with a view to their long-term implications. It is important to know whether the development is a one-off, time-critical project or (at the other extreme) a core development likely to be maintained through many revisions.

- *Non-functional requirements*. Designers often concentrate on what a system does rather than how easy it is to use, how reliable it is likely to be, how quickly it will operate, etc. As stated in Chapter 1, it is the non-functional requirements that will, increasingly, become the differentiating factor.

5.3   DESIGN METHODS

Once it is clear what the key issues are, there are many methods and techniques available to help designers record and reason about their ideas. Before cataloguing some of the better known methods we need to define exactly what a method is and what it does. Our definition is as follows:

> Method: an organised collection of notations, techniques and formal or semi-formal procedures for carrying out one or more of the major lifecycle activities. The method will identify the deliverables and prescribe the form or the notation in which they will be produced. Different methods will often be found to share common notations and techniques.

To select appropriate methods for specific applications, we have to ensure that we have an understanding of what software design methods are available, and what their capabilities and limitations are. Furthermore, it is important to choose design methods for the various classes of problem encountered, against some established criteria that relate to the environment in which they are to be used (e.g. ease of use, cost, compatability with other systems, etc). *The STARTS Guide* [NCC87], published in the UK by the National Computer Centre, gives a good example of how methods and tools can be categorised and rated against objective criteria.

5.4   PROBLEMS OF SOFTWARE DESIGN METHODS

Given that good design relies on the ability, experience and intuition of good designers, there seems to be little point dwelling on design per se. There is, however, some value in looking at the technology to support the software designer, although it is first necessary to appreciate the difficulties that exist in attempting to describe current design technologies. These problems fall typically into four areas:

- Diversity.
- Classification.
- Visibility.
- Accuracy.

Diversity

The sheer number of methods, notations and tools is such that no list of them can ever be complete. New techniques are developed by individuals and companies quite quickly, and many are not widely publicised. Many methods used are derivatives of other more well known ones, and it is often the case that an organisation will customise a method by using a subset of the original techniques or by adding on extensions. These extensions are either borrowed from other methods or are of the 'homebrew' variety. Investigation has also shown that technology usage is substantially different in various countries. Published methods, well known in the United Kingdom, for example, may not be known at all in the USA and vice versa. The same is true across Europe, where similar methods have been developed in different countries: Merise in France, Dafne in Italy and SSADM in the UK all fulfil a similar design method requirement but are respective national standards. The European community initiative to develop a Euromethod for software development may help in this area but has yet to come to fruition.

Classification

Once methods have been identified, the next problem is one of classification. Various criteria are used to describe the different approaches, and grouping together the results of an investigation always results in overlapping or exceptions being discovered. Hence no classification is ever likely to be perfect.

Visibility

The third problem area is that it is often difficult to find out exactly what actual current practice is. There is a definite reluctance on the part of many organisations to give information regarding how they develop their software. This is probably due to the fact that a significant amount of software development is not achieved by very organised and disciplined approaches, and also that those organisations who believe that they are using the *best* methods do not necessarily want to tell their competitors what they are using. Those organisations and departments which *do* volunteer information tend to demand anonymity and a high level of confidentiality. It is noticeable that, in the USA, the general attitude is different and visibility is not nearly so much of a problem.

Accuracy

Having discovered an organisation or individual that purports to using a particular method, this does not necessarily imply that they do so. Some people believe that if they draw dataflow diagrams during the design phase, they are then *using* SSADM, for example. Thus the level of some people's understanding concerning the large number of available methods, etc. can lead to major inaccuracy in reporting.

In truth, there is little substantive evidence that the adoption of systematic design methods actually improves the quality of the end product. The authors' observations across a wide range of projects would suggest that benefits do accrue but that they are rarely measured against any objective criteria. Rather, they rely on a clear understanding of how and why the methods chosen are used.

5.5   CURRENT TRENDS IN SOFTWARE DESIGN

Current practice is very much to follow the traditional lifecycle model, hence the emphasis in this chapter on this type of method. Most organisations, that are using anything, are currently using some form of one of the methods described later in this chapter (with their own omissions and additions). However, many people are now moving away from the idea of the waterfall lifecycle in favour of other ways of managing software production. The use of alternative lifecycles (notably the evolutionary model) is evident, if not yet widespread.

Along with this, more people are now becoming interested in design paradigms which shift the emphasis from 'what functions must the system perform' to 'what data needs to be manipulated in the system'. Design approaches that support this, such as object-oriented design, are becoming more accepted.

Software tools (CASE) are increasingly being used (or, at least, purchased for use) within software development organisations. Although some individual tools are now quite complex, most integrated tool-sets and software development environments are still at a relatively infant stage.

A few organisations are professing to use formal, mathematically-based design methods but the true numbers involved, especially in the case of production software, are very small. Recent surveys have shown such methods to be very much reserved for specialist purposes such as ensuring integrity in safety- and security-critical systems.

In the data processing application domain, fourth generation languages and the term 'rapid prototyping' are becoming more and more common. These types of application (e.g. payroll, ledger, etc.) tend to be fairly well defined, and current prototyping tools lend themselves more easily to this sort of development than to real-time applications.

The overall trend does seem to be towards these newer ideas of data orientation, integrated tool support and more rigorous specification techniques. Movement is slow, however, and there is much work to be done and many people to be convinced before all of these ideas can be said to be current practice.

5.6   NOTATIONS USED IN SOFTWARE DESIGN

This section describes some of the most used notations, many of which are required when following one or more of the methods described in the next section.

Data flow diagrams

A Data Flow Diagram (DFD) shows the various processing elements in a system, the data flows between these processing elements, and the major stores of data within the system. DFDs are typically used to show both the current or desired, logical or physical flow of data in a system. One diagram may be decomposed into further levels of diagrams to show greater amounts of detail.

Figure 5.1 shows an example of a DFD with activities contained in the circles (the processing elements) and labelled data flows between them. There is no indication in the DFD of sequence or ordering, simply what the data is and how it is manipulated.

Data structure diagrams

A Data Structure Diagram (DSD) describes how a data item may be decomposed into smaller data items. At the highest level, an entire object might be represented, for example, a birth certificate document. This may be decomposed into separate fields; name and date of birth, for example. The

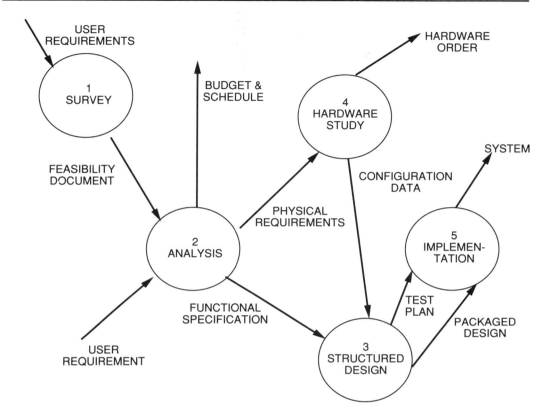

Figure 5.1 An example of a data flow diagram

date of birth might then be decomposed further into specifying the format of date that is expected; dd/mm/yy, for example. DSDs are typically drawn diagrammatically as an inverted tree. This representation of a DSD is shown in Figure 5.2, along with the textual structure for a design based on it.

Entity relationship diagrams

Entity Relationship (E-R) Diagrams are used to show the type of relationship existing between different entities in a system. These relationships may be 'one to one', 'one to many' or 'many to many', for example. Typically, the entities are represented by boxes, and the relationships denoted by different types of arrowhead on lines which interconnect the boxes. For example, a double arrowhead may denote a 'many' relationship. The boxes will normally contain the name of the entity in natural language, which would then be described more fully in a data dictionary. This type of E-R

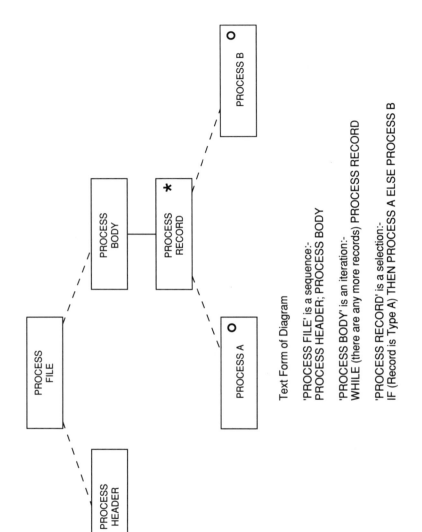

Text Form of Diagram

'PROCESS FILE' is a sequence:-
PROCESS HEADER; PROCESS BODY

'PROCESS BODY' is an iteration:-
WHILE (there are any more records) PROCESS RECORD

'PROCESS RECORD' is a selection:-
IF (Record is Type A) THEN PROCESS A ELSE PROCESS B

Figure 5.2   An example of a data structure diagram

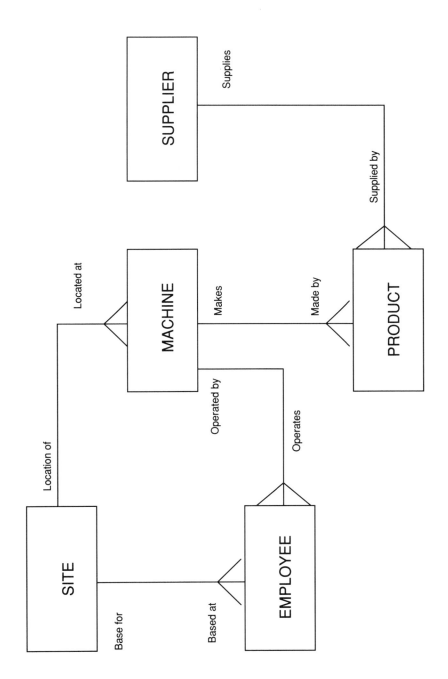

Figure 5.3   An entity relationship diagram

diagram is illustated in Figure 5.3. An alternative set of symbols consists of rectangles which denote the entities and diamonds which depict relationship types. Lines connect the rectangles and diamonds to link the entities to their appropriate relations.

Entity life histories

Entity Life Histories (ELH) are diagrams which depict how the entities in a system are created, modified and deleted throughout their life. Three different-shaped boxes are used to show processes which in some way create an entity, modify an entity and delete an entity. These boxes are connected by directed lines which link the possible processes that may follow each other. By tracing through an ELH, it is possible to cross check that, for example, no items of data are created which are never modified or deleted. ELH diagrams may typically be used in conjunction with data flow diagrams, from which the processes may be identified.

Figure 5.4 gives a defintion of the ELH symbols and a typical ELH diagram. The symbols used and the form of the diagrams vary from method to method (e.g. SSADM uses JSP notation).

Flowcharts

Flowcharts represent a structure of a program or system, with emphasis on control flow and the primitive actions performed by the program or system. The data structuring of the system is not addressed at all. Flowcharts consist of a set of boxes of various shapes, interconnected by a set of directed arcs. The arcs indicate the flow of control, while the box shapes represent different types of action or decision. Within the boxes, any notation can be used to describe the action or decision. This notation can be natural language, some form of pseudocode or even high-level language. In this latter case, tools which derive code directly from the flowcharts have been available for several years. In general, however, flowcharts can readily give rise to poorly structured (i.e. difficult to maintain) software.

Figure 5.5 illustrates one of the many ways of drawing a flowchart. System states are given in the boxes, and actions are associated with the connecting arcs. An alternative representation is described later in this chapter under the SDL method entry.

HIPO diagrams

Hierarchical Input, Process, Output (HIPO) diagrams, can be used to capture the hierarchical and interdependent relationships in a system in an uncluttered manner. HIPO was developed and refined by IBM. It captures the essence of top-down decomposition by enabling its users to break down

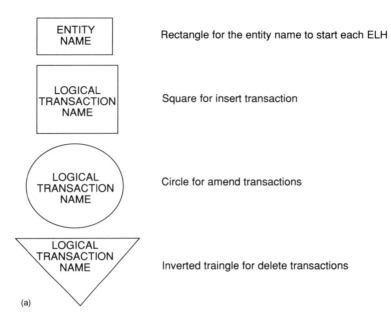

Figure 5.4(a)   The symbols used for entity life history diagrams

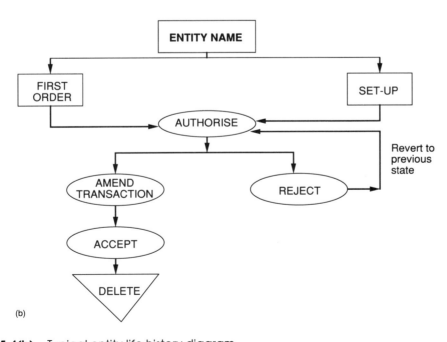

Figure 5.4(b)   Typical entity life history diagram

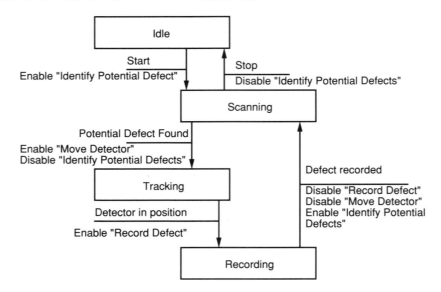

Figure 5.5 An example of a flow chart

a top-level view of a system into more refined lower-level views, without having to include logic details. HIPO uses a simple set of symbols, although the diagrams produced for large systems are difficult to change and check for consistency.

Petri nets

Petri nets provide a way of modelling concurrent systems graphically. A Petri net consists of a set of symbols which represent inputs, outputs and states. The symbols are linked with lines which show the possible changes of state that may occur, and the inputs that must be present to trigger the state changes. A particular feature of Petri nets is that, once a system is expressed in this form, the net can be used to explore certain properties of the system, such as deadlock and unproductive looping. Thus the diagrams (or rather the theory that underpins the diagrams) allow the behaviour of systems to be usefully exercised. Petri nets have been extensively used in the design of operating systems, although they have found less favour for more general applications, primarily due to their complexity. Figure 5.6 gives an example of a Petri net. The circle ('place') on the left of the diagram is marked showing that the transition from place 1 to place 2 can take place. The transition to place 3 cannot 'fire' as all input places must be marked first. Examination of the possible order of transitions is one way of using a Petri net as a design aid.

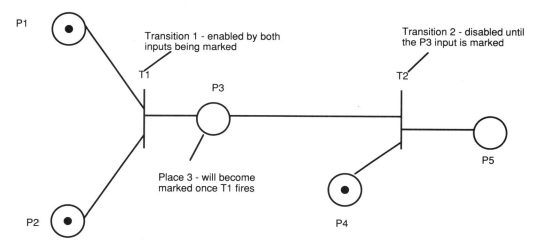

Figure 5.6   An example of a Petri net

Pseudocodes and structured English

Structured English and pseudocodes are notations resembling programming languages, used for program design. A pseudocode usually incorporates the control flow primitives of a programming language, but combines these with a narrative prose description of the computation to be carried out. An example might be:

```
while
    not end-of-file
do
    process the next character.
    ——
    ——
    ——
etc
```

State transition diagrams

State Transition Diagrams (STDs) are used to describe systems in terms of finite-state machines. An STD is essentially a directed graph (rather like a flowchart) which shows the possible states of the system as nodes, represented by boxes, and the possible changes that may take place, represented by lines joining the nodes. Often the events that trigger the state changes are annotated on the diagram. As with Petri nets, an STD diagram is underpinned with a sound theoretical base that enables formal analysis, although the complexity of practical application limits this virtue.

5.7   MAJOR METHODS IN CURRENT USE

This section outlines five of the better known and established software methods being used across the industry. More specialised or less mature but potentially important methods are also covered in this section but in less detail. No particular preference is implied in this choice of methods to explain—each one provides a good example of how a particular application can be tackled.

JSD

The Jackson System Design (JSD) method is based on modelling the system plus its environment in the real world and transforming this logical view into a physical system via a number of well defined steps [Jac84]. It prescribes a series of steps and notations to use. The method is very flexible and, like most of the currently well used methods, there is no mathematical basis behind it.

The JSD method consists of three phases, which are summarised below:

1. *Modelling.* This phase attempts to model both events and actions. *State vectors* are identified. In JSD terminology, a state vector is the collective term for the data owned by a process. *Entity Structure Diagrams* are also generated during this phase. A JSD action is an event whose occurrence must be recorded by the system and about which the system has to produce outputs. Each action has a definition and a number of attributes. Figure 5.7 shows the types of diagram that are used in this modelling phase.

2. *The network phase.* The network phase develops the rest of the specification for the system, apart from that which was derived from the modelling phase. *Network diagrams* are produced which describe processes, data streams and data flow.

3. *Implementation.* The Implementation phase is when the processes and the data are fitted on to the available processors and memory. In JSD, this is achieved via a bottom-up technique, called *program inversion*. This converts a process into a subroutine that can be called by whatever other process supplies its input data streams.

- *Source.* This method originated from and is supported by Michael Jackson Systems Ltd, (MJSL), now part of LBMS.

- *Application areas.* JSD has been successfully applied to both data processing and real-time applications.

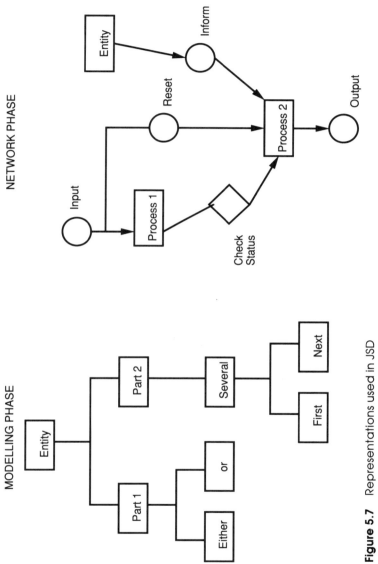

Figure 5.7   Representations used in JSD

- *Lifecycle phases covered.* JSD covers analysis and design stages of the conventional lifecycle. It is compatible with Jackson Structured Programming, which guides the implementation stage.

- *Known users.* There are too many to mention individually although an annual user group hosted by MJSL is is attended by approximately 100 people.

- *Known tool support.* Includes: Speedbuilder Workbench (MJSL), RTD (Scicon UK), PDF (UKAEA Harwell).

- *Training, maturity and other information.* JSD was first published in 1983, and is well known. Training and consultancy is available from MJSL and seems to be regarded as of good quality by those who have received it.

MASCOT

The Modular Approach to Software Construction, Operation and Test (MASCOT) method consists of six stages [Wic79]. The method emphasises dynamic behaviour and details both logical and physical design. It incorporates a template/component feature which supposedly aids component re-use and a run-time kernel to support the method. It also encourages module independence and communication between modules by promoting the rigorous definition of interfaces. MASCOT has close links to ADA and hence to Ada Programming Support Environments (APSE), into which defence departments have put significant effort. This entry is based on MASCOT 3, which will generally be referred to as simply MASCOT. MASCOT 3 is a significantly revised version of the method. The six stages of MASCOT can be summarised as follows:

1. *External requirements and constraints.* This first stage establishes the general requirements and external constraints. It involves consideration of the functional specification of the system, the hardware environment for the system, the development system to be used, and all external interactions with the required system.

2. *Design proposal.* This stage is concerned with producing a top-level design proposal. This is a more formal description of the top-level application software design with the system template partially established and the system components partially introduced. Each component is described functionally, and its contribution to the system requirement is specified. The relationship between the components and the interactions identified in stage 1 are also explored and Figure 5.8. shows a top-level design in MASCOT using its concept of actions, channels and pools (ACP). A

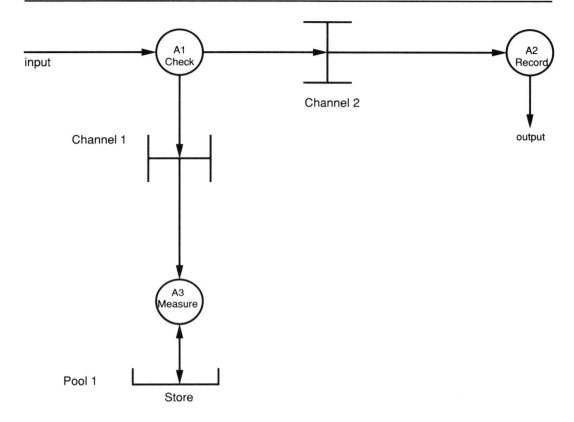

Figure 5.8 A MASCOT ACP diagram

initial study of the internal interaction between components is also undertaken.

3. *Network decomposition.* This stage is concerned with progressive decomposition of the system in terms of MASCOT networks. This involves reaching the element level with network templates being introduced.

4. *Sequential element decomposition.* At this stage, the elements identified in the previous stage are further decomposed into sub-elements. These sub-elements should be to a level that allows straightforward implementation in the next stage.

5. *Implementation.* This is the programming stage, resulting in code generation for each element and sub-element templates. Typically, access procedures are written to implement the interface specifications.

6. *Test.* The final stage is concerned with integration and the acceptance testing of the software, and often results in some degree of design rework. This stage subdivides into the definition of tests, which should correspond to the test requirements identified throughout stages 2, 3, 4 and 5, and test execution, when all the previously defined tests are run.

- *Source.* MASCOT is now in the public domain, but was developed by RSRE (Malvern) with the support of the Ministry of Defence.

- *Application areas.* The MASCOT method is specifically suited to real-time applications.

- *Lifecycle phases covered.* MASCOT encompasses the design, implementation and testing stages of the conventional lifecycle. Coverage of the latter is a feature that makes MASCOT appreciably different from other similar methods.

- *Known users.* Include: US defence establishments, NATO defence establishments, UK Ministry of Defence, BT.

- *Known tool support.* Includes: Context (Systems Designers Ltd), Perspective (Systems Designers Ltd), MASCOT 700 (Software Sciences Ltd and Ferranti Computer Systems).

- *Training, maturity and other information.* A number of training companies provide courses for MASCOT.

SDL

The CCITT Specification and Description Language, known as SDL, is primarily, as its name suggests, a language that can be used to specify the behaviour of systems [SDL88]. However, SDL can also be the basis for a method of documentation to represent a complete system description or specification. For both this reason and the fact that SDL is used to a significant extent by the CCITT and its member organisations in telecommunications applications, it is considered here as a method, rather than a notation.

SDL may be used to represent, at various levels of detail, the functional properties of a system. The functional properties consist of some structural properties, and some behavioural properties. Hence a range of representative forms are used in SDL, see Figures 5.9 and 5.10. Behaviour should be taken to mean the reactions to received signals or inputs, performing tasks and sending signals or outputs. SDL is based on the theory of finite-state machines and is therefore well suited to all systems whose behaviour can be effectively modelled by an extended finite-state machine. The state transition part of an SDL specification is shown in Figure 5.9 along with the queue-handling mechanism used between processes. The structural properties are represented by block diagrams (Figure 5.10) that include details of interfaces between the blocks.

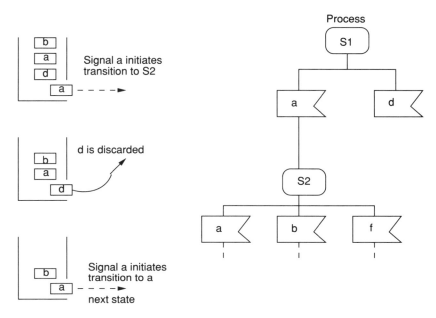

Figure 5.9   Input queue mechanism of a process

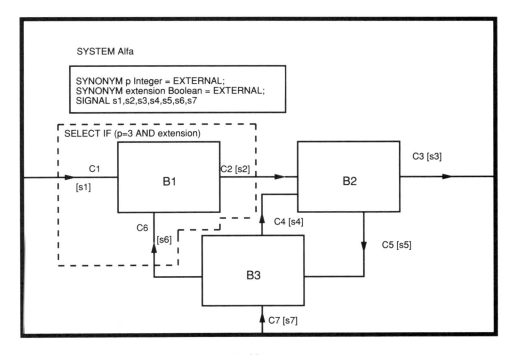

Figure 5.10   A system block diagram in SDL

SDL provides a means of describing a system with various degrees of formality, from just the use of SDL constructs with natural language, to the combination of formal statements of defined types and operators with the SDL constructs.

SDL has two different forms, one of which is a graphical representation based on a standardised set of symbols, while the other is a textual phrase representation using program-like statements. Both forms are based on the same semantic model and represent the same SDL concepts.

- *Source.* Study groups of the CCITT first began work on SDL in the early 1970s with the first recommendations emerging in 1976. The CCITT have revised the language many times since those early days, based on users' experiences. The 1988 version of SDL is a mature standard.

- *Application areas.* SDL was principally designed for use within the telecommunications industry, although it may be applied to any system that can be effectively modelled by finite-state machines. SDL is intended for applications where control flows and parallelism are important and is not suitable for purely serial, data-flow dominated applications.

- *Lifecycle phases povered.* SDL can be used for specification of requirements, and as a design representation. It was also intended to serve to document the final design of systems. Due to its formal notation, an SDL specification allows automatic code generation, and hence implementation.

- *Known users.* Usage within the telecommunications industry is very wide, including British Telecom and Swedish Telecom. Use of SDL has not penetrated very far outside the telecommunications organisations, although this may change as the international standards organisations become more and more important.

- *Known tool support.* Owing to its specialised area of application within the telecommunications domain, most users have developed their own in-house tools. A tool called SDT is available from Telelogic Europe SA. SDT and a similar tool—Geode—is available from Verilog.

- *Training, maturity and other information.* SDL is a well-tried CCITT standard and should be regarded as mature.

SSADM/LSDM

The Structured Systems Analysis and Design Method (SSADM) is a set of structured techniques in a framework of steps and stages [Ash88]. During these steps, a large amount of both graphical and textual documentation is produced. LSDM is a proprietary version of the method, from Learmonth

Burchett Management Systems. This similar method was developed from the same root as SSADM but, as time has passed, the two methods have diverged. LSDM will not be detailed any further here. The following basic principles of SSADM (version 3) are shared by many other modern structured methods:

1. The underlying data structure is important throughout the method.

2. The basic approach is to design in terms of data flow and transformation.

3. Three different views of the system are developed:

   - Logical data structure.
   - Data flow and transformation.
   - Changes in data over time.

4. Both top-down and bottom-up approaches are used.

5. Users are involved with the development from the earliest stage.

6. Formal Quality Assurance (QA) reviews are held at the end of each stage.

7. The products of each SSADM stage form much of the project documentation.

8. No mathematical basis currently exists underpinning the method.

The six stages that constitute SSADM are summarised below, although it should be noted that, in practice, some stages may proceed in parallel:

1. *Analysis of system operation and problems.* The steps within this stage involve constructing initial physical DFDs and some logical data structure for the current system. A problems/requirements list is also developed during this stage. At the end of the stage, the results of the investigation are reviewed.

2. *Specification of requirements.* This stage attempts to lead the analyst away from the constraints of the current implementation, by developing a logical view of the current system. A number of different *business systems options* (BSOs) are then drawn up, which express the requirements in the various ways that the system might be organised. Based upon the selected BSO, a detailed specification of the required system is built up and checked extensively.

3. *Selection of technical options.* At this stage, if new computer equipment will be required to implement the proposed option, enough information should be available to compile a list of possible configurations. Each option is costed out and the potential gains and losses weighed up. The final solution is then chosen.

4. *Logical data design.* In this stage, the logical data design is built up to include all the required data, and then a relational analysis technique (normalization) is used to group data items and cross check the data definition defined in stage 2. The logical processes developed in stage 5 are checked against the final data design to ensure that all the data required by the processes is present.

5. *Logical process design.* The definition developed in stage 2 is expanded to a sufficient level of detail so that an implementor could build the system. As described above, the processes are also checked against the final data design.

6. *Physical design.* The complete logical design, both processes and data, is converted into a design that will execute in the target implementation environment. This may include *tuning* the design on paper, to meet the performance needs of the system. The detailed program specifications are then used to code the programs in a chosen language.

- *Source.* In 1980, the UK Government started a procedure to select a structured method to use as its standard for all computing projects in UK government departments. SSADM was the product of this selection process, and overall responsibility now lies with the Central Computer and Telecommunications Agency (CCTA). The National Computing Centre (NCC) has a collaborative agreement with the CCTA to publish the official reference manual. The current issue of SSADM is Version 4 and the method is currently being standardised within the BSI—the impact of this would be that SSADM could be mandated as a design method. The proprietary version of SSADM, available from Learmonth Burchett Management Systems, is known as LSDM.

- *Application areas.* SSADM was originally selected with data processing applications in mind.

- *Lifecycle phases covered.* SSADM fully covers the analysis and design stages of the lifecycle and also impinges on the requirements identification.

- *Known users.* Known UK users include the following: UK central government, UK local government, Central Television, British Gas, Automobile Association, British Telecom.

- *Known tool support.* Includes: EXPRESS (Scicon UK), Excellerator/SSADM and Systems Engineer.

- *Training, maturity and other information.* Many commercial training organisations now offer training courses for SSADM, and LBMS naturally provides training for LSDM. SSADM is relatively new to the scene although it is evolving and maturing rapidly. Training companies may be formally accredited, and practitioners can gain a certificate of proficiency. Similarly, a conformance scheme exists for the appraisal of support tools.

Yourdon

The Yourdon method for structured analysis and design is a set of notations and techniques with guidelines for their effective use. Yourdon involves the production of a number of models. It is emphasised that the method only suggests these different models, and does not impose their use. Flexibility is thus a distinct feature of Yourdon. The main models are listed and described below:

The feasibility study models

These feasibility models are both textual and graphical descriptions of the current system, thus providing an analysis phase for the method. The four specific models suggested are:

- *Current implementation model.* This model describes the current system as it physically exists. It models the existing system's implementation.

- *Current essential model.* This is designed to model the current system but, unlike the previous model described, this model is independent of the actual implementation. It is a logical rather than physical picture of the current system.

- *Preliminary context model.* This is a first attempt at modelling the system with respect to its environment. It shows how the main function of the system interfaces to the outside world.

- *Preliminary cost model.* This model is typically an economic analysis of the problem dealing with the costs of the proposed system.

The system model

The system model is more concerned with the design aspects of the required system, and may be broken down into five components, as follows:

- *The essential environmental model.* This is designed to highlight the requirements for the system's interaction with its surroundings. The notations suggested to be used during this stage are context diagrams, event list and a data dictionary.

- *The essential behavioural model.* This is intended to illuminate the required responses of the system. Data flow diagrams, entity relationship diagrams, process specifications and a data dictionary are the notations suggested for use in this stage.

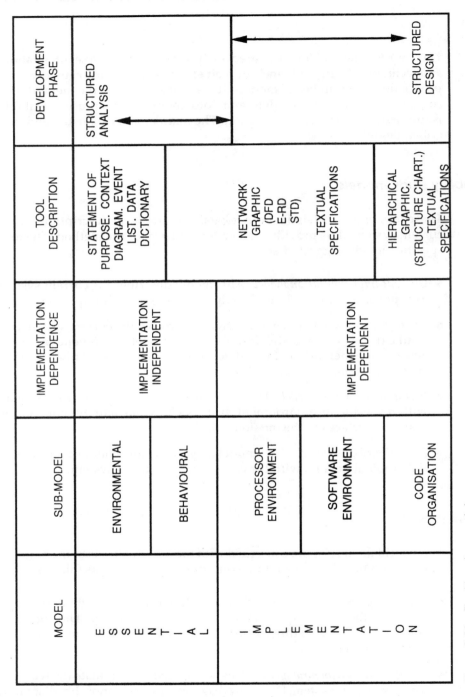

Figure 5.11 The Yourdon model

- *The user implementation model.* This is intended to illustrate the user's view of the required system. The suggested tools and notations include DFDs and state transition diagrams and screen generators.

- *The systems implementation model.* This model is intended to illustrate the various technical implementation choices available. Again, DFDs and STDs are recommended.

- *The program implementation model.* The idea of this model is to aid detailed program design. The notations recommended during this stage are structure charts, DFDs and module specifications.

The context of the above set of models is described in Figure 5.11 which shows how they fit into the development phase and how they can be implemented.

- *Source.* The Yourdon method originates from Yourdon International Ltd, headed by Ed Yourdon himself, a well known authority on the subject.

- *Application areas.* Yourdon has been widely used by different organisations for both real-time and data processing applications.

- *Lifecycle phases covered.* Yourdon covers feasibility, analysis and design stages of the conventional lifecycle.

- *Known users.* There are many users of Yourdon.

- *Known tool support.* Teamwork (CADRE), Yourdon Workbench (Yourdon), Analyst Toolkit (Yourdon), Software through pictures (IDE) and Excellerator/PT.

- *Training, maturity and other information.* The method is now quite mature, having first been seen in 1975. Training, documentation, on-site support and consultancy are all available from Yourdon.

5.8   EMERGING APPROACHES

Over recent years a number of promising design approaches have emerged that break away from the traditional lifecycle model. These approaches, outlined below, have yet to achieve the level of acceptance of Yourdon, for instance, but promise to be useful additions to the range of options open to the designer.

Object-oriented design

Object-oriented design (OOD) is based around the ideas of information hiding, inheritance, data encapsulation and abstract data types [Mey88]. The approach views all the resources, such as data, modules and the system

itself, as objects. Each object encapsulates a data type inside a set of procedures, which manipulate the data type. Using this idea, designers can create
their own abstract types and map the problem domain into these designer-
created abstractions. This contrasts with the more traditional idea of mapping the problem domain into the pre-defined control and data structures
of an implementation language. The object approach is much more natural
than process-oriented design techniques since various different kinds of
abstract types may be created in a design process. Consequently a designer
can concentrate on the system design without worrying about details of the
data objects used in the system.

It should be noted that OOD is a fairly 'loose' concept at present, and that
there are many different opinions of how it should be practised. No clear
well defined methods for following the object-oriented approach have yet
been published, although such a design method might typically involve the
following four broad stages:

1. Identify the objects and their attributes.

2. Identify operations on the objects.

3. Establish the interfaces.

4. Implement the operations.

Some authors have regarded the OOD paradigm as revolutionary in concept, other see it as little more than good design practice with well defined
modules and interfaces. It is, however, at least a significant change in development approach. In the object-oriented environment, the emphasis shifts
from 'how do I write my program?' to 'how do I use what is already here
to solve my problem?'. The object-oriented programming (OOP) languages
offer support for this different emphasis by way of features like inheritance,
dynamic binding, and polymorphism, and tools such as browsers, inspectors and high-level debuggers. Some current examples of OOP languages
are Smalltalk, Simula, Eiffel, C++ and Objective C.

In summary, object-oriented approach is a rapidly growing technology,
which emphasises software reusability and exploratory programming. Much
work is still required before it is widely considered useful for the delivery
of production software. There is also some potential for a very much higher
degree of reuse as far as software development is concerned with objects
being the base components from which systems can be constructed. It is,
however, too early to say whether this notion will translate into practice.

Prototyping

The aim of prototyping in a software development environment is to
speed up the development process by presenting the user with a working

demonstration version of the final product early in the development process [Har87]. Thereafter, development effort is concentrated on refining this agreed product. A major benefit of this approach is the potential opportunity to clarify (or modify) the user's requirements. The prototyping process is therefore interactive and user-driven. It is also flexible, since there is no fixed plan of activities that must be followed for the whole development but a cycle of plan, develop and review (see Chapter 3). In this respect, prototyping is the antithesis of the current structured development methodologies. Some research efforts are, however, trying a combination of the two approaches, prototyping and SSADM, for example.

Prototyping is now becoming an accepted way of developing data processing type applications. Fourth generation languages (4GLs) are now widely used both as a development language and as a design tool and it is feasible to create working applications (albeit not always fully functional) in a matter of a few weeks. Currently, prototyping tends to be best suited for agreeing the user interface, such as screen formats, report layouts, and data entry procedures.

The level of user involvement during prototyping should be very high. Consequently, there is a better chance of getting the user to agree when the requirements are right at an earlier stage. One of the dangers of this approach is, however, knowing when to stop refining and when to agree on the final system. It is quite usual for the user to see the first demonstration version, and then to demand the reason why they cannot begin using it immediately. Another problem can be getting the amount of user interaction required. If sufficient commitment is not forthcoming from the users, then prototyping is unlikely to be successful.

Because of the flexible nature of prototyping, it is often said that the approach is impossible to manage. Although project management can be difficult, a responsible development team with an effective project control system can overcome this. Also, project management of the traditional structured methods has not always been a great example by comparison.

Typical examples of current 4GL's and similar environments in use include: Focus, Ingres, Inset, Oracle, Powerhouse, Pro-I and, Ramis II.

In summary, current fourth generation tools do provide very good non-procedural facilities not found in traditional third generation languages. Quite complicated reports can be generated through a simple statement, in many 4GL systems, for example. Lack of precise definition and standardisation are the main problems with 4GLs and they often lack procedural facilities, which may be a disadvantage. Generally, if the problem matches the assumptions in the tool's pre-defined non-procedural facilities, then the user may well save appreciable development time. If this is not the case, conventional programming may be a better alternative.

Rigorous/formal design methods

The introduction of formal methods in software development would be a major step towards improving the software engineering process [Jon86]. Formal methods can be described as rigorous engineering practices based on mathematical foundations. They can provide a means of expressing system designs concisely and unambiguously, and in a way that the behaviour of systems can be explored through formal logical manipulation. One commonly cited drawback of formal methods is that they are not easily assimilated by humans, and require highly specialised knowledge/experience. Conversely, the notations used are generally more easily manipulated by a machine than, for instance, English text.

Evidence of current actual use in production software activities, is limited although some succesful field trials of formal notations as parallel specification checks have been reported recently.

There are several styles of formal specification methods, some of which are more applicable to particular types of problems than to others. The Vienna Development Method (VDM) and Z specify systems by describing how operations alter the state of the system. This is more effective when specifying intensive data manipulative problems, but less so for event-driven systems.

The Calculus of Communicating Systems (CCS) and Communicating Sequential Processes (CSP) specify systems using concurrency and event sequences. They are well suited for describing the behaviour of event-driven concurrent systems, but cannot readily handle data-driven applications.

OBJ represents a third class of formal notation, based on the idea of abstract data types (ADT). It describes the properties of objects in a system without using the concepts of state or storage. A particular benefit of OBJ is that specifications written in it may be executed and thus exercised.

The Language of Temporal Ordering Specification (LOTOS) is a good example of a composite notation. It combines the ideas used in CCS with those of the property-oriented ADT concepts of OBJ. LOTOS is also an ISO Standard and has been used as a notation for specifying communication standards such as X400, ROSE, MHS, etc.

Of the organisations professing to use formal methods, IBM have well publicised their use of Z on the CICS project and have also indicated that it has led to a 9% saving in system maintenance costs. Even so, evidence of practical application of formal techniques is not widespread. VDM has been cited as being used by some departments of Standard Telephones and Cables (STC), the General Electric Company (GEC) and Rolls Royce and associates. Z has been used by both IBM and British Telecom, the latter using it as a means of verifying critical system components.

In summary, it would seem as if, despite acceptance of their principles, formal methods are not widely used and in some organisations, are not even known about. The most widespread use of such rigorous techniques has so far been in safety-critical applications, and MOD contracts for example.

5.9   OTHER DESIGN METHODS

For completeness it is worth noting that there are many other design methods which fit (roughly) into the conventional lifecycle development approach [Pet81]. They are mostly hybrids of each other and some are more well known than others. This section briefly outlines some of these methods. As stated earlier, no particular value judgements are made here. Some of the methods mentioned below are rapidly gaining acceptance (e.g. IEF).

Arthur Young IEM

Arthur Young Ltd market an Information Engineering Methodology (IEM), aimed at business systems, from analysis to implementation. Their main product which supports the methodology is known as ADW. The company also offers training courses and consultancy.

EPOS

EPOS is a fixed notation which represents a design both in textual and graphical form. It interfaces well with CORE and leads to generation of Fortran, Pascal or Ada code. EPOS is also usable in conjunction with JSD, Yourdon and an object-oriented design approach. It originated from the Institute for Control Engineering and Process Automation in Germany. Its first use was in 1980. EPOS -R, -D, -S, and -O form an integrated toolset, which some would call an IPSE, to support the method. Software Products and Services Inc (USA) are also connected with the method. EPOS tends to encourage the use of large amounts of storage. It supports the ideas of decomposition, abstraction and data refinement, but leaves the separation of design and implementation to the discretion of the designer.

HOS

HOS originates from Higher Order Software, an American company, but is supported in the UK by DMW Group (Europe), of London. It claims to formalise functional specifications, and uses three means of expression:

● Control maps.

● Structure design diagrams.

● Pseudocode.

The maps are represented by a machine-processable language called AXES. No particular application seems apparent and there is no support for concurrency and other real-time factors. Its main areas of use, in relation to the lifecycle, are concerned with problem decomposition and design. All of its visible use seems to have been in the USA. Tool support is available via the USE-IT toolset, which runs under the VM operating system. The method puts emphasis on consistency and correctness issues and strict hierarchical operating system modularity is imposed. It also has strong links to the idea of abstract data types. It has been in existence for a number of years.

IAI/Statemate

The Israel Aircraft Industries/Statemate method provides a model for the design of embedded systems. The system is described from structured, functional, and behavioural points of view, using Statemate languages. It claims that precise graphics formalisms exist for each viewpoint, and is similar to Hatley's concepts of architecture, process and control models. The strengths of the method include formal semantics underlying the graphic formalisms. *Statecharts* are also used to describe finished state machines at different levels of detail. A support tool is used to execute the models. However, costs are reputed to be high, and there is little in the way of training materials or texts.

JMA/IEF

The James Martin Associates (JMA) Engineering methodology is a graphics-orientated discipline. It is specifically aimed at analysis and design through to the code generation for business systems. It is used by JMA in-house and by their business consultants. A tool known as the Information Engineering Facility (IEF) is available to support the method. During the analytical stages of a project, various *business models* are created. These are refined during the design stages to produce *technical models* that will be used for translation into system code.

PDL

Program Design Language (PDL) is a form of structured English used for software design and, specifically, the detailed design stage of the lifecycle. It was developed by Caine, Forber, and Gordon Inc of the USA, but is supplied in the UK by Warren Point Computers Ltd in Hertfordshire.

Its application area is described as very wide, but is recommended for *large* projects. It was widely used in the States but has only recently appeared in the UK. PDL is easily integrated with a step-wise refinement design approach.

SADT

The Structured Analysis and Design Technique (SADT) provides support for functional decomposition, working on a 'divide and conquer' principle. It uses a number of models, each of which consists of a hierarchy of diagrams describing a system from a particular viewpoint. SADT uses a graphical language with well developed syntax, semantics and pragmatics. The main relevant lifecycle phases are functional specification and design and the main application area is real-time. One known user is the European Space Agency. It originated from SoftTech, but is now supported by Micromatch in the UK, who offer a training course. The original documentation is reputed to be very good and the method has been successfully employed on a number of projects. Tool support is in the form of ASA and Specif-X, and also IDefine from Micromatch. SADT does support concurrency, but does not promote abstraction. The method is quick and easy to learn, but the tools are reckoned to be more difficult to use. Some users of the method apparently reported difficulty bridging the gap between requirements and design.

SAFRA

This is a diagrammatic and machine-processable method, whose acronym expands to Semi-Automated Functional Requirements Analysis. It actually relies upon a combination of CORE and MASCOT. It was developed by British Aerospace and was directed particularly at real-time applications. The only known user found was BAe themselves, and they are producing a dedicated workstation for SAFRA. Another tool called PSL/PSA also exists. SAFRA covers aspects of requirements capture, design and code generation. It could, however, be regarded as simply a customised combination of CORE and MASCOT.

SARA

Systems ARchitects Apprentice (SARA) is a collection of modelling and evaluation tools and techniques which support structured hierarchical methodology. It uses Petri-net type notations and provides interfaces specifically for the language PL/1. It originated from UCLA, and is aimed at real-time digital systems. It professes to cover the lifecycle right from requirements through to testing of the implementation. Research has suggested, however, that SARA may not be available or supported in the UK. Similarly, although tools such as an analyser, simulator, compiler, checker and database exist, they may also be difficult to obtain in the UK.

SREM

The Software Requirements Engineering Methodology (SREM) is part of the Distributed Computing Design System (DCDS), which is a set of interrelated methods, languages and tools to support the entire software development path. It consists of a Requirements Statement Language (RSL) to specify relationships between the objects comprising a system. There are four main steps:

- Translation.

- Decomposition.

- Allocation.

- Analytic feasibility demonstration.

It was designed for original use in US ballistic missile defence systems, and is marketed by TRW (US). It really has the specific aim of aiding requirements definition of real-time embedded systems and has been used by a number of companies in the USA. A tool called Requirement Engineering and Validation System (REVS) provides consistency checking.

STRADIS

STRuctured Analysis Design and implementation of Information Systems (STRADIS) is a method which uses both diagrammatic and textual notation in an attempt to capture requirements and specify the functionality of the required system. It is based on the notation introduced by Gane and Sarson. Its application area does not particularly support concurrency or real-time aspects. It originates from MacAuto, and MacDonnell Douglas are also associated with it. Tool support is in the form of Stradis/Draw which is an aid to producing the diagrams required by the method. Lifecycle phases covered include analysis, design, functional specification and implementation.

5.10   A DESIGN CHECKLIST

The final section of this chapter elaborates on some of the key design issues identified earlier. For each of the key issues, two or three of the most important questions that need to be answered are identified.

Constraints

- Does the customer require specific design methods and tools to be used? (This point is particularly relevant to, for instance, Government and European Commission projects where methods such as SSADM and Mascot are mandated.)

- Do particular procurement practices constrain selection of design methods and tools? (Standards such as ISO 9000 and Def Stan 00-55 are prerequisites to many contracts.)

- To what extent does existing hardware/software constrain design options? (For example, processor and memory constraints, predefined operating system or language.)

Customer expectation

- Is it important to have customer input through the design process? (This may imply the need for a systematic, preferably graphical, method to record design design decision.)

- How much validation is approporiate to meet customer needs?

Type of System

- Does the system fall into a recognised category for which there are proven design methods? (For example, transaction processing, database, real-time.)

- What external interfaces will the system be required to work to and have the interfaces between project elements been clearly identified?

Type of application

- Will it be straightforward to update the delivered system? (Embedded systems may require more validation pre-release than a system that can be evolved.)

- Is the system prone to change or are the requirements clear?
  (The adoption of a waterfall or prototyping approach should reflect this.)

- What size is the system likely to be?
  (This will have implication on the organisation required to carry out the design and the level of support that needs to be put in place.)

Project environment

- Is there sufficient experience of the application of the chosen method/tool?
  (Experience shows that the learning curve on a new method usually negates any potential benefit.)

- What size of team is required for the project?
  (Some methods do not scale up, or down, particularly well.)

- Are design walkthroughs and reviews held?
  (This should be part of quality procedures and should include reviewers from outside the design team.)

- Are standards in place to define the design process?
  (For instance, is a common method prescribed for all team members, is design documentation kept under configuration control?)

Whole lifecycle view

- Are there specific acceptance criteria laid down for the project as a whole?
  (The choice of design approach may impact, positively or negatively, on their achievement.)

- Is there any obligation to support the system after release?
  (If a system is to have a long life, changes are inevitable and these need to reflect back on the initial design.)

- What level of documentation is required?
  (Some methods/tools create and, sometimes, manage a large volume of design documentation.)

Non-functional requirements

- Are there performance requirements on the system?
  (This question goes beyond design, but design choices have significant impact.)

- What level of reliability is required in the final system?
  (This can be related to the amount of effort invested in design verification.)

- Is usability of the final system a key factor?
  (Design approaches which include prototyping are more appropriate if this is the case.)

5.11 SUMMARY

Software is unlike the other components of any system in that there is no widely accepted way of defining either the product or the process of its creation. This, compounded with the complexity of many systems, leaves the software designer in an unenviable position.

At the root of the problem lies the fact that software design depends, in the absence of any firm theoretical basis, on skill and experience. In its current state 'software engineering' is a term applied to practice rather than a science. The fact that a great deal of practical experience of software development has been amassed over the last 20 years has sustained the industry to date and we now have available a wide range of special purpose tools and methods to support the designer. The reason for the diversity of available methods is partly that different applications require differing approaches and partly due to the particular views of the method's inventors as to what constitutes good design practice.

Nonetheless, a number of themes have emerged—common techniques such as data flow analysis are used in several methods and all methods seek to document and support the intellectual process, leading to the production of high-level code.

The greater part of this chapter has concentrated on outlining some of the most widely used methods, such as Yourdon, SSADM and SDL. In addition, some emerging design approaches, notably object-oriented, formal notations and prototyping, have been examined.

5.12 REFERENCES

[Ash88] Ashworth, Caroline M. (1988) Structured systems analysis and design method (SSADM), *Information and Software Technology (UK)*, **30.3** pp 153–163.

[Har87] Harwood, Keith (1987) On prototyping and the role of the software engineer *ACM SIGSOFT SE Notes* **12.4** p 34.

[Jac84] Jackson, M.A. (1984) The future for structured methods: JSP and JSD, *State of the Art Report: 12:1, Structured Methods* (Pergamon Infotech).

[Jon86] Jones, Cliff B. (1986) *Systematic Software Development Using VDM* (Prentice Hall International).

[Mey88] Meyer, Bertrand (1988) *Object Oriented Software Construction* (Prentice Hall).

[NCC87] National Computing Centre (1987) *The STARTS Guide*, volume 1, 2nd edition.

[Pet81] Peters, Laurence J. (1981) *Software Design: Methods and Techniques* (Yourdon Press).

[SDL88] CCITT Study Group IX (Switching and Signalling) (1988) *Recommendations on the Functional Specification and Description Language (SDL) Z.101 to Z.104*, CCITT, Geneva.

[Wal85] P. Wallis (editor), *State of the Art Report: the Software Development Process* (Pergamon Infotech) pp 130–135.

[Wic79] Wickens, R.F. (1979) *MASCOT, A Modular Approach to Software Construction Operation and Test*, Civil Service Dept, Central Computer Agency, Issue 1.

6
Testing

We often find out what will *do by finding out*
what will not do
Samuel Smiles

In general terms, software testing is the process of locating and fixing errors. The testing phase of software development is usually seen as the activity immediately before the release of the finished product—the final series of checks for errors.

This definition is in line with current practice, but ideally testing should be associated with *all* phases of a software development, and should deal with the validation of requirements and verification of specifications as well as the correct operation of the final code.

In a perfect world, tests would ensure that all software faults were removed before release. There are several reasons why this is, at present, an unrealistic aim. First, there are literally millions of possible paths through even straighforward software. It is not viable to test each and every possible combination of input, state and output. Second, changes will always be required throughout the life of the software. No test will be once and for all and every change (whether it is an update or a fix) will carry with it the possibility of new and previously untested behaviour being introduced.

Given that complete testing is not viable, the question of how much testing should be done and where it should be applied is an important one. For instance, projects in safety-critical areas where the integrity of the software is paramount (such as military or space applications, medical software and systems in 'fly-by-wire' aeroplanes) should be tested much more rigorously than, say, a simple word-processing package. This implies that there is not a global 'best practice approach', and the extent of testing relies, to a very large degree, on the particular application.

The budget (both time and money) allocated to testing is often regarded as that which is left over at the end of the development phase. The correct amount is difficult to set in advance, as it varies from one organisation to another and, within an organisation, from one project to another. Even so, testing should be planned at the outset rather than left to the end. It is only by keeping careful records of time actually spent on testing and the effectiveness of that testing that managers can start to build up the necessary profile of testing needs in their area.

This chapter aims to cover the key issues in organising and measuring software testing along with the main techniques available to make the process more systematic. A brief checklist at the end of the chapter gives some of the questions that need to be addressed.

6.1 WHY TESTING MATTERS

Most testing is currently seen as a necessary evil after the implementation stage of a software project. Despite increasingly complex systems being produced, there seems to be little corresponding increase in the effort devoted to testing or in awareness of test techniques. As a result of the widely held 'code then test' attitude, any overspending in the earlier stages of a project will tend to squeeze the testing stage, with the result that less time and effort are available for carrying out these activities.

This is borne out by recent surveys, which indicate that there are relatively few practitioners in UK industry who consider that enough time is allowed for testing—typically 15% of time and effort is considered a generous allowance. To learn how the software industry, as a whole, is likely to develop in this country, one should look at the examples set by leading companies in the US, where testing is treated with as much respect as any other part of the software engineering discipline and a 40% allowance for testing is widely accepted. Thus it is not surprising to find that much of the research and development in this area is done in the US by leaders in the field such as Myers, Beizer and Hetzel.

Quite apart from the lack of time and effort allocated to testing is the fact that the level of automation routinely applied in this phase is low compared to, for instance, the design phase. This is surprising, considering that a range of tools is available and they inherently provide the repeatability and accuracy required in testing.

In the UK, a report commissioned by the Department of Trade [PA85] suggests that the application of software testing tools would result in overall savings of 9–18% for system development. The report also states that any investment in software tools would provide a return of two- to threefold in terms of time and effort saved

Looking at the current situation in a little more detail, we can list some of the most common approaches to testing used throughout the industry.

Ad hoc (random) testing

This usually involves the programmer, or a tester, attempting to crash the software under test. It may be at the unit or module level, but is usually at system level. Typical strategies are deleting fields which do not exist, providing incorrect input or using knowledge of the hardware or environment to force a crash. This cannot be considered proper testing for a number of reasons:

- The whole process is unsystematic. It is rarely planned and controlled.

- The inputs and predicted outcomes have not been documented.

- If a suspected error is found, the random nature of the inputs, the lack of documentation and possible use of non-printing characters mean the effect cannot be replicated.

- Any suspect output must be checked with the design documentation to ensure that it is incorrect and not what the user actually specified.

There are certain occasions when this type of testing can, however, provide benefits. For instance, when the range of likely errors is well known. Furthermore, the use of capture/replay tools can help overcome some of the inherent shortcomings of the method by introducing a measure of repeatability.

Even so, it is stressed that, at best, random testing is only as good as some of the more methodical approaches (such as domain testing) and at worst it lures the tester into a false sense of security about the extent to which the software has actually been examined.

Manual testing

This involves a set of test cases which, to be run, are keyed into the computer by hand. This is very widespread throughout the computer industry, and is still seen as the way to execute a suite of tests. However, the resources tied up, and the random errors introduced by incorrect keystrokes, mean that this approach is only acceptable for fairly trivial test suites. An automated execution system is essential to ensure reliable results, as the test cases can be built up and stored for later regresssion testing. Thus tests become another vital project resource, like documentation.

Programmers testing their own code

This in itself is not an ideal practice, although the programmer probably knows the code better than anyone else. The problem is a psychological one —since testing is essentially a destructive process many programmers find difficulty forming the correct mental attitude towards code which they have produced [Mye79]. Another associated problem is that the code may contain errors due to the programmer's misunderstanding of the specifications. If this is the case, it is likely that the programmer will have the same misunderstanding when attempting to test their own program. The ideal situation is for separate test teams to undertake the responsibility of testing. Where this is not possible or desirable, and the development team and test team overlap, roles and responsibilities must be clearly defined.

6.2   SOME SYSTEMATIC APPROACHES TO TESTING

When attempting to characterize the testing process, four basic process models can be identified. These demonstrate how test techniques have evolved over the last 35 years [Het88].

- The demonstration model.
- The destructive model.
- The evaluation model.
- The prevention model.

The demonstration model

Used mainly between the late 1950s and late 1970s, the goal of this model was to demonstrate, by execution, that the software satisfied its specification. The approach is similar to that used in acceptance testing. It was from this period that the phrase 'code and test' originated, and for many this still remains the approach. The objective was to show that the program did not contain any faults.

The destruction model

After the introduction of microprocessor technology in 1973 there was a desire for a more comprehensive software approach. The period from 1979 to 1982 is identified by its concentration on detection of implementation faults. Myers [Mye79] defined testing as 'the process of executing a program with the intent of finding errors'. The emphasis had shifted from demonstrating that the software had no faults to an assumption that faults existed and had to be detected.

The evaluation model

The increase in professionalism associated with software testing throughout the 1970s, and the recognition of software engineering as a professional discipline, led to methods which viewed testing as an integral part of the lifecycle. This period, from 1983 to 1987, is marked by the aim of detecting requirements, design and implementation faults, mainly by analysis, review and testing activities. Where the analysis and review activities are combined with one of the two previous models the process is sometimes called verification, validation and testing (VV&T).

The prevention model

The first two models above are regarded as phase processes because they are mainly execution based and happen as a distinct testing phase in the software development. The third model is viewed as a lifecyle process because it views testing as an integral part of the lifecycle.

The final model, also a lifecycle process, is very similar to the evaluation model but with the goal of preventing requirements, design and implementation faults. This model was introduced in 1987. The difference between the evaluation model and the prevention model is the increased prominence of test planning, test analysis, and test design activities. Review and analysis activities are required to support test planning and design, or to evaluate test products. For example, a review of software requirements to support software design for testability would be included as part of the overall project plan.

The major benefit of this approach is improved quality of software specification and designs. Incompleteness, ambiguity, inconsistency and incorrectness are revealed when these faults are still relatively cheap to correct. By building behavioural models of the software it is possible to identify the need for requirements and design changes at an early stage. This model reflects the current best practice in this area.

6.3 PROBLEM AREAS IN TESTING

Quite apart from the general problem of insufficient resource being devoted to testing, there are a number of technical problems that need to be recognised. Some of the main ones are outlined below.

Configuration management

The need for rigorous configuration management is especially strong in the testing process as a large volume of information (both documentation and code) is generated which must be accurately tracked and filed. Some of the special problems encountered in testing are:

- New tests are being constantly created.

- Tests are updated, but the old versions have to be retained.

- Different test versions need to be recalled.

- Test cases must be able to be related to results.

- Problem report forms must be stored.

All of this information must be stored for a long period of time as the project goes from the development through to the maintenance phase. Updates will have to be added at each new release of the system and test data must be kept for all distributed versions and variants.

Gathering statistics from such a large volume of paperwork, or conducting searches to attempt to pinpoint common problem causes, is both time-consuming and labour intensive. To date, a large part of the software industry has failed to use even widely available tools (such as database packages) to hold this information.

With such a configuration management problem it is not surprising that test cases, stubs and drivers are often discarded under the misconception that they are 'one-off programs'. More information on configuration management is given in the next chapter.

4GLs and DP systems

Fourth Generation Languages (4GLs), such as Ideal or Natural, and data processing (DP) systems (based on languages such as COBOL) have traditionally been used to produce databases, financial and banking systems. There are an estimated 70–75 billion lines of COBOL code alone in the world.

Some of this code has been in place for many years in paygroups, tax offices, etc. To transform this poorly documented and unstructured code to modern structured code would be prohibitively expensive; hence the need for continual upgrades to meet changing requirements. This is not a trivial task on what are usually large systems and requires stringent regression test requirements. Often the only formal testing that is practical is system and acceptance testing, where the tester's goal is to show that the software performs to its specifications.

As well as the problem of volume, the increasing use of 4GLs presents a testing problem. The nature of these languages does not readily permit a direct mapping of some of the techniques available in other areas of software production (see Section 6.4).

Furthermore, the testing tool market is aimed predominantly at the high-integrity, real-time applications. Fewer testing tools which operate on modern DP languages are available.

Some tools, such as Automator, can be used to aid in the testing of these types of system. However, research is still needed into the impact of 4GLs on testing.

Real-time and networked systems

There are several reasons why these systems present a challenge to the tester. The first is, again, sheer complexity: the number of test paths in even a small network are too numerous to cover in practice. A large networked system has so many possible combinations of events/actions, etc. that only a small number can be exercised.

The need to test within real-time constraints compounds the problem and means that software elements under test often require a sophisticated test environment to accurately assess their likely performance *in situ*. This is especially true of software to be used in remote or embedded systems (e.g. satellites, undersea switches) or for communication over a variable delay network (e.g. protocol software elements connected over packet-switched networks).

There are a host of other areas that present a challenge to the tester (e.g. parallel, object oriented and reusable software). Those mentioned above are only the tip of the iceberg.

6.4 TECHNIQUES FOR TESTING

It is not possible to discuss all the techniques currently in use throughout the software industry; there are far too many to do justice to here and several excellent texts are already available (see [Bei83], [Het88], [OU86]). We concentrate here on introducing some of the key strategies for effective testing of both code and requirements/designs.

Testing, in the broadest sense, covers a range of activities which parallel the conventional development lifecycle and for each development stage there is an associated test activity. Figure 6.1 shows the main categories of tests carried out through the lifecycle. Once initiated these test activities may span a number of development stages. The most effective testing should start as early as possible in the lifecycle, at the requirements or system design stage.

Techniques employed at the early lifecyle stages

Formal methods, symbolic execution and theorem proving

Although formal proofs are expensive, requiring highly trained staff, they have been used effectively on safety-critical projects (e.g. in the rigorous design of nuclear power systems). However, until tool support becomes widely available, formal languages are unlikely to enjoy wide use as a replacement technology in the software industry, although the 'shadowing' of the critical modules of a software design with a formal version, which can be used to verify consisitency in critical sections, is a viable and effective mechanism for early testing.

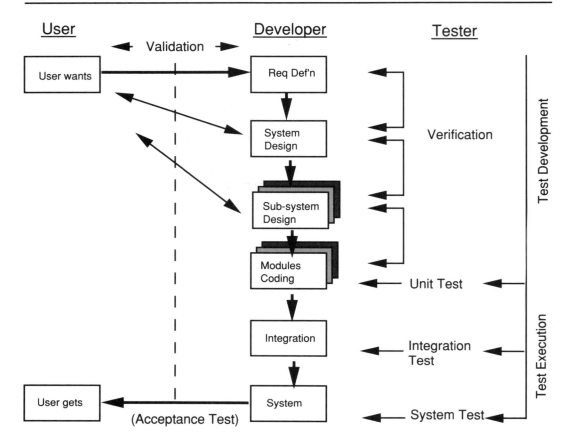

Figure 6.1   Some of the main test operations during development

Reviews, walkthroughs and inspections

These are probably the most widely used techniques, but suffer from the fact that they are really only as good as the people involved. Even so, they have been shown to be highly cost effective.

The definition of *inspection*, according to [IEEE83], is: 'A formal evaluation technique in which software requirements, design, or code are examined by a person or group other than the author to detect faults, violations of development standards and other problems.'

Research into the effectiveness of inspections in a wide range of application areas has concluded that: 'While inspections do not eliminate testing, they can significantly reduce the testing effort because inspections are from two to ten times more efficient at defect removal than testing. Furthermore, regardless of the application or the language, you can expect inspections to find from seven to twenty major defects per thousand noncommented lines of source code and to find major defects at cost of one to five staff-hours.'

The actual inspection process has a number of people (in defined roles such as presenter, reviewer, chair) examining software requirements, design or code for faults. Often, checklists are used as they have proved to be useful to the reviewers as memory aids and help ensure conformance to set standards.

The *walkthrough* is a manual execution of a section of code. The developer talks through the operation of the code with other developers, testers, etc. who concentrate on the detection of flaws in the code.

The *review* is less formal than an inspection and is used within the design team (within peer groups) to examine requirements, design documentation or code.

Validation of requirements

It is vital to maintain traceability between requirements and test cases. One approach to this is the use of test matrices. These matrices map system requirements onto test cases to ensure that all the stated requirements are tested. This mapping encourages the testability of requirements to be considered early in the lifecycle. The *requirements validation matrix* built up in this approach entails the listing of each requirement to its associated test cases. Often, the same test case is used to test more than one requirement, and some requirements need more testing than others.

There are a number of immediate benefits from using a requirements validation matrix, the most valuable of which is the discipline of forcing test cases to be designed for each requirement. This helps to eliminate untestable requirements. The matrix can easily be made part of a higher-level overall testing plan, and can be updated as the testing proceeds. The decomposition of attributes which are untestable into lower-level attributes which are testable forms the basis of Gilb's Quality Attribute Specification [Gil88].

One final, and very powerful, technique for validating requirements is prototyping (see Chapter 5). This is especially useful for user-interface design but requires careful control (i.e. is the prototype to evolve or is it just for demonstration?).

Current techniques in operation at code level

Static analysis of programme code via:

- *Complexity measurement.* There are a number of metrics that have been developed to characterize the complexity of software, the most common of which is the McCabe complexity metric [McC76]. This is based on the control flow structure of the program and indicates how complex a piece of code is. There is a certain amount of debate as to exactly how useful the measure is, although there is growing evidence that testing the most complex modules first is the most efficient way of finding errors in the shortest time. Also, the metric roughly equates to the number of test cases needed. In practice tools are essential for such analysis.

- *Coding standards.* Many organisations have guidelines on how code should be written. Typical examples are nesting of if-then-else constructs, use of global and local variables or multiple exits from loops. With defined coding standards, the code is more easily understood by the testing team. Given that 65% of coding and logic design errors are found at the module testing level [Mye79], stringent coding standards can help the testability at the module level by, for example, limiting the size of a module to, for instance, between 30 and 50 executable statements.

Dynamic analysis of program code via:

- Functional ('black box') testing. In black box testing, the internal structure and behaviour of the code is not considered at all. The objective is to find out solely when the input–output behaviour of the program does not agree with its specifications.

- Structural ('white box') testing. This is one method of determining how much of a section of code has been tested, and how much remains. The coverage is gauged in terms of statement, branch or path execution (these are defined later in this section). Tools are essential for practical 'white box' testing.

Equivalence partitioning

This is a black box testing technique which is concerned with identifying classes of inputs over which the behaviour of the software is 'similar'. For example, if a program is expected to produce a certain output when an integer between 1 and 100 is input, and different outputs depending on whether the integer is less than 1, or greater than 100, then the equivalence classes will be integers less than 1, 1 through 100, and greater than 100. The idea of equivalence partitioning is that inputs in the classes are representative of the class as a whole and that the amount of test data required can thus be minimised.

Boundary value analysis

This technique is one step on from equivalence partitioning with test cases being selected from the separate classes. The technique explores the boundary values of the input classes. For example, consider a module requiring an integer in the range of 1 to 20. Useful test cases would be 1, 0, –1, 19, 20, 21, –20. Other test cases could be a large integer, a decimal, a very small integer, and so on. Clearly with a module requiring anything but the most basic input, exhaustive testing of this type is not possible. The problem then moves from 'what test cases can be derived?' to 'what are the most useful test cases?'

Code coverage

Estimating the amount of code which has been executed by a particular set of test data is one way of gauging the effectiveness of the tests, and can also help to derive new test cases. Three types of coverage are:

● *Statement coverage.* This is the weakest type of code coverage and is simply the number of statements executed by the test data. It can be done manually, by inserting PRINT commands into the code under test or with tool support. Since a single statement may contain more than one condition (such as a boolean if A or B) this type of coverage must be considered weak in terms of test completeness.

● *Branch coverage.* Branch coverage requires that program branches be executed during testing. This gives a more thorough measure of the test coverage than statement coverage, but is difficult without tool support. Branch coverage is heavily supported by Beiser [Bei83] and is a practical alternative to path coverage.

● *Path coverage.* This requires that all the program paths be executed during testing. Since the number of program paths in a module can be very large, complete path testing may not be possible. Path testing is, however, the most rigorous type of coverage. Without tool support, estimating the coverage is time-consuming.

To illustrate the differences between statement, branch and path coverage consider the following example (figure 6.2). In the diagram the diamonds represent decision statements. The loop has to be executed ten times. To complete 100% statement coverage takes only three test cases. These will execute the paths 1,2,4,9,10; 1,2,3,7,8,10 and 1,2,3,5,6,10. For 100% branch coverage, an additional three test cases are required—namely 1,2,3,5,10; 1,2,3,7,10 and any other test case involving the loop returning to 2. For 100% path coverage the number of test cases is 5^{10}!

In practice, tools are required to assess code coverage—inserting statements into the code can be done manually, although it is very tedious. Tools such as TESTBED do this automatically.

Data flow analysis

Data flow analysis is the checking of the actions on a data item. There are a number of obvious errors which could occur:

● Item defined but not used.

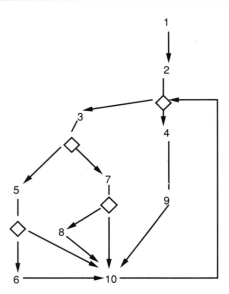

Figure 6.2   An example of logic to be tested

- Item defined and then redefined with no intervening usage.

- Item referenced but undefined.

Data flow anomalies can also happen between calling modules. This inspection process should pick up many such data flow errors. Members of an inspection team can be instructed (usually with a checklist) of the likely errors to look for. This checklist can be periodically updated to reflect the types of errors being discovered. Some tools provide data flow analysis support, for example, MALPAS, SPADE and TESTBED.

Random and ad hoc testing

In random testing the tester or an automatic test driver derives and executes tests from information given on the module or system. The results still need to be checked manually, and this is time-consuming, laborious and unreliable.

Another aspect of random testing is often apparent at the system test level. A member of the test team (or another individual) subjects the system to a series of random inputs and ad hoc tests. This cannot be considered proper testing for reasons stated earlier in this chapter. It is, however, a significant show of confidence in a system when the designer will allow such a random onslaught to take place—several designers cite the throwing of a cat at the keyboard as the ultimate test of a system's survivability!

Regression testing

Regression testing is 'selective retesting to detect faults introduced during modification of a system or system component, to verify that modifications have not caused unintended adverse effects, or to verify that a modified system or system component still meets its specified requirements' [IEEE83].

Usually it is not practical to re-run the entire test suite, and so selective retesting must occur. It is at this point in the system lifecycle that the configuration management of previous test cases/harnesses, etc. will pay such large dividends. If a test suite has been built up with tool support (such as TESTA) then the regression testing process is greatly eased. If not, it is a laborious, tedious, time-consuming and unreliable process.

One of the major problems when performing regression tests is how much of the previous tests need re-running. Hetzel [Het88] suggests the use of a retest planning matrix, which maps test cases onto system modules and is produced during initial development and testing. The *retest planning matrix* helps the tester to decide what test cases need to be re-run, but can only work if all the original test cases, harnesses, etc. are available. The *retest planning matrix* therefore encourages the saving of test data for further use.

Volume testing

Volume tests stretch the system to its design limits with large volumes of transactions, data, etc. Typical tests could be to edit a very large file, submit a program containing thousands of modules to the compiler, and so on. It can be useful to push the system not only to its design limits, but past them. That way any inadequate safety margins may be detected. This type of testing is likely to be expensive in terms of planning and execution time, and so a long series of volume tests is probably not feasible.

Stress testing

Stress testing differs from volume testing in that the system is subjected to heavy loads, though not necessarily reaching any of the system limits. Myers [Mye79] draws an analogy with a typist. The volume test is whether or not the typist can deal with a very large document. The stress test determines if the typist can reach 50 words per minute.

Stress testing may not be applicable to some batch programs or perhaps a compiler program. However, in real-time applications it is essential to subject the system to as much stress as possible. Some situations which seem a remote possibility and not worthy of examination can take place under certain conditions. For example, it may not seem realistic that all the users of a large computer would want to log in at the same time, but this may happen when the system is brought back into service following a crash.

Syntax testing

Although syntax testing can be used at module or subsystem level, it is better suited to systems testing. Syntax testing explores the ability of the system to accept or reject variations on the correct input strings. The technique involves identification of the components, or features of a system, which are amenable to syntax testing. The syntax must be formally defined, for example in a Backus–Naur form [Bei83]. This syntax is then tested in a similar manner to compiler checks. The number of tests which may be generated is very high, so it is useful to have some form of automation.

Consider the example where an input string might be in the form of AABBcc. Now let AA be one or two alphabetic characters from A to G, BB is one or two alphabetic characters from a to g, and cc is an integer from 0 to 99. This simple syntax form can now be used to produce test cases, such as AA or GGgg99. It also highlights the fact that the input string AA is different from Aa. This may or may not be an error.

Some research has been carried out comparing the effectiveness of different software testing strategies (e.g. [BS87]). The techniques that have received most attention have been code reading, functional testing and structural testing. The overall conclusion to date is that none has been found to be a convincing winner in terms of total errors found, although the *types* of errors found varied for each of the techniques.

At integration, system and acceptance test levels, structural test techniques, such as path testing, are usually impractical. The tester must rely on black box techniques such as syntax testing and boundary value analysis.

In contrast, functional testing has been found to be the weakest approach in terms of gauging how completely tested a particular module is. To redress the balance, [Nta88] states that 'purely structural testing strategies provide no guidelines for selecting the actual values with which to execute a test path.' This implies that no one single test technique, no matter how well installed or supported, can hope to capture all errors. A broad understanding of all the approaches and when they should be applied is required.

6.5   TEST STANDARDS

The software industry in general has been slow to adopt test standards, and it is only in comparatively recent times (the last few years or so) that a coherent drive towards quality in this area has taken place. The adoption of standards, such as [IEEE86], will not guarantee the quality of software produced under it, but it does go some of the way towards enforcing a disciplined approach to software production—standards should be seen as a minimum level of achievement rather than as a ceiling to aspire to.

Use of standards, in conjunction with other control mechanisms (such as version control), can provide a framework to help ensure that:

- Errors are detected and corrected as early as possible in the software life-cycle.

- Project risk, cost, and schedule effects are minimised.

- Software quality and reliability are enhanced.

- Proposed changes and their consequences can be quickly assessed.

6.6   WHEN TO STOP TESTING

Since the time available for testing is limited (and complete tests are not viable), it is vital to ensure that the most important tests are carried out first. In this way the best use is made of limited time and the maximum number of errors are found. The straight line on Figure 6.3 would be the likely rate

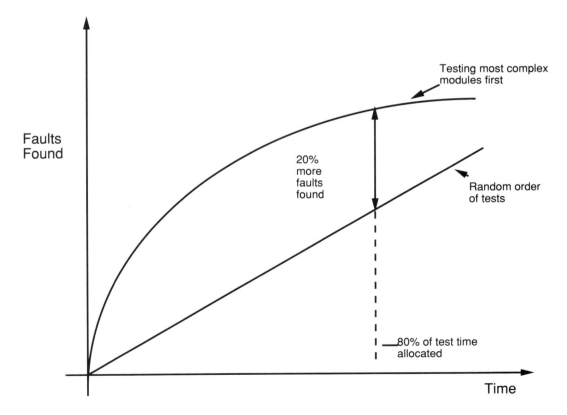

Figure 6.3   Typical rates of fault discovery

of errors found with time, assuming random distribution of errors. In practice, however, errors are often concentrated and by correlating errors found with code measures, an order of testing (e.g. most complex first) can be imposed. In effect this pushes the straight line towards a more optimised curve of early detection of errors.

The decision as to how much testing is enough is often made as a result of money or time constraints, rather than a predetermined target level. It is essential to keep track of the testing process so that the information to enable the decision as to when testing ceases to be cost effective can be objectively taken. Some of the measures which can be used to provide this objectivity are:

- *Rate of error detection.* The rate of error detection should provide an indication of how the test process is proceeding. The plot is lifecycle related, but often an initial peak and trailing off indicate that one type of testing (like unit testing) should be completed and another (such as integration testing) initiated. The graph will then show another increase in error detection as new types of errors are discovered.

- *Code coverage.* As part of the test plan, a minimum degree of code coverage may be specified. For example, target values could be 100% statement coverage, 80% branch coverage and 50% path coverage. Testing ceases when these goals are realised. Again the actual values vary according to application. For realistic application of these approaches tool support is essential. Another useful application of code coverage is in measuring the effectiveness of test data.

- *LoC (lines of code).* This was once the classic measure of program size. However, it does not take into account program structure (a large structured program may be easier to understand than a smaller unstructured one) or comments. Despite these obvious shortcomings it is still widely used as a measure of program size.

- *McCabe's essential complexity metric.* This is calculated by counting the number of branch statement in a piece of code to indicate the number of paths (and hence complexity of the code). This can be useful in highlighting those areas of code which may prove difficult to test or maintain. The graph in Figure 6.3 shows the common finding that the more complex modules in a system (i.e. those with the highest McCabe number) should be tested first as they are the source of most errors.

All of the above measures can be used to give an indication of where errors are likely to be. This opens the way to schedule testing to investigate the most problematical modules first, hence maximising the effectiveness of the time spent on testing. Also, the coverage measures explained earlier (branch, statement and path) give a reasonable basis for test completion targets.

6.7   TOOL SUPPORT

One of the themes that has run through the introduction to test techniques is the need for automation. Several kinds of software tools can be used to improve the efficiency, accuracy and repeatability of testing. As with design tools, this is a fast moving area which we will no more than outline here.

Structural testing tools

These tools, such as TESTBED, analyse the control flow structure of the program. The most obvious advantage of automation at this level is taking some of the tedium out of the testing process, with an increase both in accuracy and in efficiency. On a higher level, the tool returns an objective measure on the effectiveness of the test data used, giving feedback both to the tester and to the manager. The tool may offer other 'features' such as:

- Complexity measurement (based on McCabe's complexity measure or similar).

- Identifying sections of code which are executed frequently, or not at all.

- Identifying coding standards violations, such as multiple exits from loops.

Regression testing tools

The area of regression testing (and the associated topic of software maintenance) has been an area of much research in recent years. Structured design and programming have eased the burden of this area of testing, giving code which is easier to maintain, but it remains a work-intensive area. Since the requirement is for a re-run of previous test cases (plus perhaps a number of new ones) automation greatly aids the process. Several tools are available which allow automated test capture and playback, such as TESTA and Evaluator.

Databases

The testing process generates a large volume of paperwork in the form of:

- Test cases and results.

- Test plans.

- Problem reports.

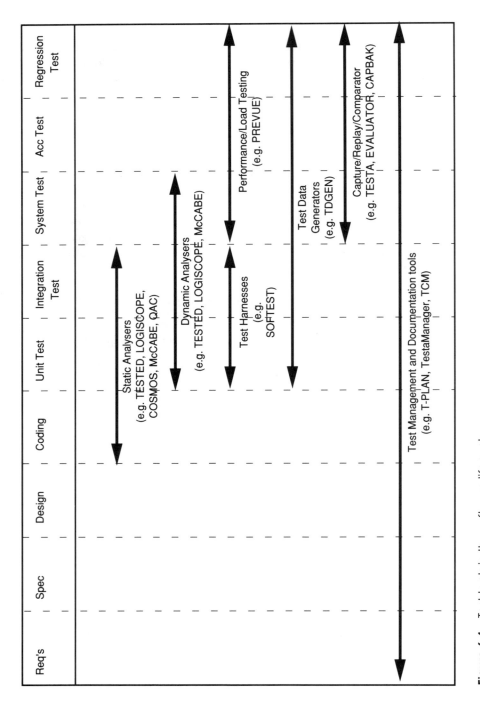

Figure 6.4 Test tools in the software lifecycle

- Problem evaluation.

- Follow-up reports.

The storage and manipulation of this information can be greatly eased by the use of a database system. Searching for a related set of reports, or deriving statistics for use by management may be performed by a series of simple tools. While no commercial tool has yet been identified which has been purpose built, database packages are widely available.

Software tools require an initial outlay in money and staff training. If the tools are used correctly this expenditure should be recouped in better-quality software being produced and, in the longer run, in increased efficiency of future test activities. A comprehensive guide to the tools that are available for software testing can be found in [Gra90], and Figure 6.4 shows what tools are available and what they cover. In practice, the production of test harnesses, etc. are essential for adequate software testing.

6.8   TRENDS AND INFLUENCES

There are a number of current trends in the software industry that seem likely to be important from a testing point of view. These include:

- Many more companies will be forced to come up to the current best industrial practice by conforming to accepted procedural and technical standards. The increasing adoption of quality systems such as BS 5750 or ISO 9000 and the take up of *de jure* standards such as the Unix operating system should increase the portability of both tools and procedures.

- Increased automation will be adopted, with testing tools accepted as the best way to test software at the module level and regression test tools helping in the later stages of the lifecycle and system.

- The use of more rigorous requirements capture and design practices should enable more errors to be located early in the development process.

- Legal and commercial pressures, with increased liability on the producers of software, may force the introduction of minimum levels of testing for certain systems.

- Newer structured programming languages (e.g. 4GLs and OOD) will have to be adopted by companies wishing to bid for certain types of contracts (e.g. defence, transaction-processing systems). This may require a change in the current test strategies.

- Other lifecycles such as evolutionary prototyping, where the customer effectively carries out acceptance tests during the development, do not follow the waterfall lifecycle model (see Chapter 3). If other lifecycles become widespread then, irrespective of technical detail, existing techniques must be adapted or new techniques developed.

- Managers will require more information in the form of metrics to discern the quality and required quantity of tests. In the near future a coherent and meaningful collection of metrics for use in the software industry may be developed.

- Automatic selection of test data from information derived from either program or specifications. Methods for achieving this, usually based on symbolic execution or data flow, have been demonstrated on small language subsets but their use at the moment is limited. It is anticipated that this work will continue, and produce tools operating on much larger language subsets.

Other topics which may provide useful benefits in the future include a test data adequacy criterion (a set of rules to determine whether or not sufficient testing has been performed), theorem provers to verify designs prior to test, cause–effect graphing, and artificial intelligence techniques. However, useful (or practical) input to the computer industry from these techniques is still some way off.

6.9   A TESTING CHECKLIST

The final section of this chapter, as in previous chapters, is a brief checklist against which any organisation can assess what it does on some of the key testing issues. In the checklist, six main areas of concern are identified, ranging from overall approach to testing though to specific activities such as planning and documentation.

Overall approach

- Are there defined test procedures in place?
  (As outlined in the main text, there are many techniques and tools available. If testing is to be carried out systematically then adoption of one or more of these is an important step.)

- Are independent test teams used?
(The potential problem of developers assessing their own software is that oversights in design can, often unwittingly, be repeated in test.)

- Are standard methods for software development (for examples, see Chapter 5) used?
(Systematic methods of development help both in defining at what stage testing should be carried and in providing a defined object (e.g. a system specification) to test against.)

Planning and organisation

- Is sufficient time and effort set aside for testing?
(As a rule of thumb, somewhere between 30% and 40% of a development budget should be allocated to testing.)

- Are test plans produced as part of the overall project plan?
(It is important not just to schedule tests but also to set measurable objectives for quality of releasable code, to decide what will and won't be tested, to define test methods, tools, etc.)

- Are tests formally reviewed and recorded?
(Much valuable data can be collected during tests, for example, where errors are found, and at what stage in the development they were introduced. This is only useful, however, if test results are logged and if all test apparatus (test cases, harnesses, etc.) are kept under configuration control so that valid comparisons can be made over time.)

- Are the responsibilities for testing clearly defined within the project plan?
(It is important to assign and define roles within the test team. Responsibility for the test plan, test case design, maintenance of test metrics, etc. has to be clearly defined.)

Documentation

- Is there a top level test plan?
(This should cover the objectives for quality, acceptance criteria, responsibilities, methods and tools to be used, etc.)

- For a large project, are there detailed test plans for each of the major phases of the project?
(A similar range of issues covered in the top-level plan need to be covered for acceptance testing, integration testing, etc.)

- Does test design follow a standard format?
  (Standards such as IEEE-829 provide a comprehensive definition of the documents that should be produced in test design.)

Preventive measures

- What checks are carried out in the requirements phase to trap errors?
  (Consideration should be given as to whether requirements are testable and acceptance criteria should be formulated.)

- What checks are carried out in the design phase to trap errors?
  (Specifications should be tested for consistency and for conformance to requirements.)

6.10 SUMMARY

Testing should not be an activity tacked on to the end of software development. To be most effective, it should be carried out as an ongoing part of the software development process: the sooner errors are found the easier (and cheaper) it is to fix them.

The view that software testing is a single stage in the development process after coding has led to the production of poor-quality software. The current industry-wide practices involve few real testing techniques or tools. Instead, sets of test data are entered manually in an attempt to demonstrate that the code under test works. Often programmers test their own code, and are caught in a conflict between creating a product and then being asked to find errors in the same product.

This situation need not exist as there are many test tools, techniques and methods now available. A recent report suggests that the application of software testing tools would result in savings of between 9% and 18% for system development. The report also states that any investment in software tools would provide a return of two- to threefold in terms of time and effort saved.

This chapter has outlined some of the main techniques for software testing and the types of tools that are available. Most of the approaches covered in the text are straightforward—they simply provide a systematic, reproducible basis for carrying out tests on software systems.

Looking beyond the improvements that can be made simply by investing in current best practice, there are a number of areas in which testing can become more effective. In the short term these include objective measures for planning tests and increased automation.

Perhaps most important in the drive for quality is the move away from error detection towards error prevention. This is supported at present by the use of reviews and walkthroughs at early lifecycle stages and potentially by the use of more rigorous specification techniques.

6.11 REFERENCES

[Bei83] Beizer, B. (1983) *Software Testing Techniques* (Van Nostrand Rheinhold).

[BS87] Basili V.R. and Selby, R.W. (1987) Comparing the effectiveness of software testing strategies. *IEEE Trans. on Software Engineering* **SE-13. 12** pp 1278–1296.

[Gra90] Graham, D. (1990) Software verification and testing tools: availability and uptake *Proc. Software Engineering '90 Conference* (Brighton) (IEE).

[Het88] Hetzel, W.C. (1988) *The Complete Guide to Software Testing*, 2nd edition (QED Information Sciences Inc.).

[IEEE83] IEEE (1983) *IEEE Standard for Software Test Documentation*, ANSI/IEEE Std 829-1983.

[IEEE86] IEEE (1986) *IEEE Standard for Software Verification and Validation Plans*, ANSI/IEEE Std 1012-1986.

[LT88] Loo, P.S. and Thai, W.K. (1988) Random testing revisited, *Information and Software Technology* **30.7**.

[Mur86] Murine, G.E. (1986) Using software quality metrics as a tool for independent verification and validation. *Proc. Conf. on Computers and Communications* (Phoenix).

[Mye79] Myers, G.J. (1979) *The Art of Software Testing* (Wiley-InterScience).

[Nta88] Ntafos, S.C. (1988) A comparison of some structural testing strategies, *IEEE Trans. on Software Engineering* **SE-14.6** pp 868–874.

[OU86] Ould, M.A. and Unwin, C. (1986) *Testing in Software Development* (Cambridge University Press).

[RTP88] RTP Ltd. (1988) *MALPAS Executive Guide* (RTP Ltd, Newnhams West Street, Farnham, Surrey, GU9 7EQ, UK).

7
Maintenance

Plus ca change, plus c'est la meme chose
Alphone Karr

7.1 INTRODUCTION

It is probably fair to say that no-one knows exactly how much any large organisation spends each year on software maintenance. There is, however, a considerable body of accumulated information in this area and we can make an informed guess. Studies that have been undertaken and published (for various organisations around the world) indicate that between 40% and 70% of all software expenditure goes into maintenance. The example of the small software company given in Chapter 1 is typical and, when taken with the anticipated growth of software production, illustrates the need to ensure that as much care is put into keeping software as is put into its creation.

This chapter provides an overview of the software maintenance process. It serves to set the background of the subject and to highlight the critical areas of concern. In addition to reviewing existing knowledge we present a vision of what lies ahead in maintenance; a combination of dealing effectively with what is given and of evolving better practices for future systems.

The next section explores exactly what is meant by the term software maintenance and why it poses a problem. Subsequent sections deal with the various aspects of the maintenance process; Section 7.3 puts maintenance into the context of the software lifecycle, Sections 7.4, 7.5 and 7.6 deal with the key parts of the maintenance process—management of the process, configuration control and change control. Finally Section 7.7 outlines a few the ways in which the state of software maintenance is evolving and Section 7.8 is a checklist of some of the key maintenance issues that need to be addressed.

7.2   THE MAINTENANCE PROBLEM

What is meant by software maintenance?

This is the first source of confusion, because different authors and practitioners hold different views [Can72]. It is not so much that they disagree about what has to be done: it is more that they argue about whether the set of operations that must be performed to keep software operational should all be described as 'maintenance' or as 'maintenance plus other things'.

Most of the published descriptions of the software lifecycle, described in Section 7.3 treat the maintenance part of it in one of the following three ways [Swa76]:

(a) as simply another activity at the end (reasonably enough), or

(b) (in diagrams) as a series of feedback lines, implying repetition of some or all of the preceding activities, or

(c) by ignoring it.

Option (a), while indisputable, conveys little understanding of what actually goes on, and will be expanded below.

Option (b) looks tidy, and correctly indicates that specification, design, etc. are indeed all part of the maintenance activity. However, it could also be taken to imply that, given a change in the specification, one would then redesign and recode the whole product, whereas, in practice, the more usual procedure is one of analysis followed by incremental change. The authors' opinion of option (c) will not be recorded.

Figure 7.1 gives a simplistic but useful maintenance lifecycle. This shows periods of intense activity (and high cashflow) when changes are being made to an existing product. Interspersed with this are periods of quiet (and lower cashflow) when the only changes being made to the product are the fixing of errors.

Given the fact that no universally agreed definition exists, we are forced to state what definition will be used here. The following is proposed:

Software maintenance is the set of activities associated with keeping operational software in tune with the requirements of its users and operators, and of all other people and systems with which the operational system interacts.

This is rather a broad definition, and so it is worth amplifying it by listing the categories of maintenance that are usually considered to make up the set of activities. There are four such categories, and where alternative names for them are sometimes used, the alternatives are given in brackets.

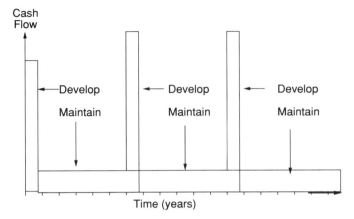

Figure 7.1 Distribution of costs over the lifetime of a product

The categories are:

● *Corrective maintenance (repair maintenance).* This involves the correction of errors in a piece of software, where an error is defined as a deviation from the specification. The prediction of the extent of corrective maintenance that any new program will require is a matter of keen interest and (so far) little progress, although a level of around 20% of all maintenance costs to fix errors is a reasonable average, based on experience in telecommunications sofware.

● *Adaptive maintenance.* This involves the alteration of a program to bring it into line with changes in its specification. Such changes may result from new user requirements, or from a change in the program's operating environment, for example.

● *Perfective maintenance (productivity maintenance).* This alters neither the specification nor the software's adherence to it, but it improves the performance by making the software consume less resources (or, at least, by reducing the overall cost of the resources it does consume). 'Resources' here include factors such as execution time and memory usage.

● *Preventive maintenance.* This final category directs its benefits towards the overall maintenance process itself. It involves making changes to the software that in themselves improve neither correctness nor performance, but make future maintenance activities easier (i.e. cheaper) to carry out.

Further to these definitions we can define:

● *Maintainability.* The ease with which a software system can be corrected when errors or deficiencies occur, and can be expanded or contracted to

satisfy new requirements—see Chapter 10 for a mechanism for quanti-
fying maintainability.

The above definitions are by no means perfect and are often blurred in
practice, sometimes by intent [GEC86]. Nonetheless they serve to illustrate
what tasks face the maintenance programmer.

Why is there a problem?

There are many reasons why software maintenance is difficult—some inherent, others due to lack of research, development and objective measurement
of the process itself.

Basically, maintenance programmers have to cope with large and
ever-increasing volumes of software, and are all too often required to
deal with systems whose documentation is ill-suited to their needs, or is
even entirely absent. Where this is true, maintenance immediately becomes
costly and tends to tie up more than its fair share of the most able
programmers.

Put another way, maintenance is difficult on a system not designed to be
maintained.

Specific sources of difficulty are:

- 75–80% of existing software was produced prior to significant use of
  structured programming.

- It is difficult to relate particular aspects of a system's behaviour to specific
  code.

- Changes are often not adequately documented.

- There is a ripple effect—typically changes to a piece of code are not
  localised.

Some of these factors are, in themselves, insoluble; they remain as difficulties that can only be eased with more sophisticated techniques for maintenance. Others are a direct result of design decisions that are made or
development techniques that are used.

7.3 MAINTENANCE IN THE SOFTWARE LIFECYCLE

In expanding on the composition of the maintenance phase, the level of
detail to be aimed at must be a matter of fairly arbitrary judgement; but from
observation it seems that there are four readily identifiable phases that a
released product goes through:

- A phase of *enhancement*, in which the specification of the product undergoes considerable alteration. (This phase is recognisable from its tendency to emit major new releases.)

- A phase of *maturity*, in which the specification remains relatively stable and the main activity (if any) is corrective maintenance. The software can be viewed as a reliable commodity in this phase.

- A phase of *obsolescence*, in which the product remains available and in use, but the ability to alter it has been lost. This phase is the precursor to technical death .

- A phase of *termination*, in which the product may still be in use, but all control has been abandoned.

It might be thought that the last two of these phases are scarcely worthy of consideration, but as outlined in Chapter 3, they are relevant to calculations of overall product cost benefits, and their initiation at the correct time is certainly a matter of economic importance to the organisation, given the resources that can then be freed.

Each of the phases has its own features and it is useful to consider the characteristics of each.

Enhancement

During this phase at least one earlier version of the product is in use, and, simultaneously, large changes are being made in preparation for the next planned release. The main concern is that the users are requesting problem fixes and minor enhancements on the version(s) they have, and the new version cannot be issued until it has fully been brought into line with the revised specification.

The user requests, therefore, must be applied to the earlier version and a new intermediate release issued. Two problems immediately arise:

- The work takes resources from the enhancement work, and disrupts its plans.

- When (not 'if') a change forces or implies a change in the specification, the enhanced specification must also be kept in step.

The resource problem is an awkward one, and one way round it is to set up a separate team to handle the changes to the 'old' product. This simplifies administration and resource control, but it suffers from three disadvantages:

- Communication between the two parties becomes more distant (even if they are physically close together), leading to difficulties keeping the old and new specifications in step *or* to a heavy communication overhead.

- There is duplication of effort, in that each team must independently be able to understand the whole product.

- There is a problem of authority which arises when each team, working from its own priorities, desires a different and mutually incompatible change in the specification.

The main danger here is in not keeping specifications in step with the operational system. In some situations any change that alters the format or semantics of the stored data is a latent problem that may not be revealed until the enhanced product is released, and users attempt to migrate to it.

Maturity

It is possible to argue with the name given to this phase, since the project may still seem to the users anything but mature, but it is nevertheless distinguished from the previous phase by the absence of further planned major enhancements. Adaptive maintenance will still occur, of course, but the main aim is probably to stabilise the product by correcting all remaining errors that are sufficiently significant.

Probably the most significant problem of this phase (although it is already present in the previous one), is that of the *deteriorating system*. Every change made to the software runs some risk of introducing a new error, and if the risk cannot be kept within bounds, the performance of the product will actually deteriorate with time rather than improve. This can be likened to a mechanical product wearing out.

Obsolescence

The onset of this phase may be triggered by any of several things:

- The loss of the only person(s) who understood an undocumented program.

- The inability to maintain the support software or hardware (e.g. a change in user needs that is beyond the inherent design of the system).

- The inadvertent loss of the source code (through fire, flood or lack of effective configuration management).

- Deliberate and rational decision.

Whatever the cause, the effect is that the software can no longer be maintained or, at least, the cost of imposing any change would exceed the cost of complete replacement.

During the obsolescence phase, activities do not cease; after all, an unmaintainable product is no problem as long as it still works. It earns cash and costs little to support. Configuration management (of the object code at least) will still be required, for example, and user support functions should continue to be provided. However, the only significant problem appears to be that of deciding when the phase should start (assuming it is by decision rather than accident).

Termination

During this phase, there is no central control over the product, and no user support, although individual users may still retain and use the product. Again, the only problem (for the central authority) is deciding when to initiate the phase.

7.4   THE MANAGEMENT OF MAINTENANCE

Managing the maintenance activity, like other forms of management, involves creating and preserving an environment which will best allow the activity to take place. There are aspects of it which are common to most or all management situations, and these will not be explicitly covered here; instead, the concentration will be on issues that particularly apply to maintenance or that give rise to particular and significant problems there. The following broad areas are considered and discussed:

- Planning and monitoring.

- The handover problem.

- Training.

- Resource control.

- Recruitment and motiviation.

- The user viewpoint.

Planning and monitoring

Planning for maintenance carries the particular problem that it is very hard to estimate the likely demand for work, since no-one knows in advance how many errors will be discovered in the software, and how many change requests the users will make. The problem is exacerbated when the planning is left until the last minute, as can happen if the developers are not to be involved in the maintenance and can therefore regard it as 'somebody else's problem'.

A further difficulty that will be encountered is the political one: requests for change may be strongly influenced by company political factors [KI84].

Planning is not a one-off activity in maintenance: projections will be revised many times during the life of a product. It should, at least in theory, become easier with time, since there will be past experience to draw on—if you know how many errors and enhancements had to be processed last year, then you have a reasonable basis for planning next year.

However, the only way to know that is to keep records: i.e. to monitor the activity. This might seem an obvious point, but for example Lientz and Swanson [LS80], in a survey of 487 DP organisations, found that only 40% had what they considered to be good data on how much time they allocated to maintenance—a very basic point. The details of what should be monitored, and how closely, will depend on the organisation and the product.

The handover problem

In those cases where a product is developed by one team and then given to another to maintain, the transfer process itself may become protracted and expensive.

It is important to have a clear set of criteria for handover—for instance, the documentation provided by the design team must help the maintainers understand the software, and the software must come with appropriate facilities to build, test and manage the constituent files in the system.

Training

The successful maintainer needs to know 'everything about everything', but that sort of statement does not translate easily into concrete training plans. In practice the most important areas in which to ensure technical competence are configuration management and code analysis techniques because the 'bread and butter' of maintenance is the location and orderly revision of existing code.

Resource control

In most of its aspects, this is a general management problem, but two aspects that relate particularly to maintenance (and to each other) will be mentioned.

The first is the question of where in an organisation should maintenance be performed. Should it be done by the same people that do development, or by a separate team? And if the latter, how separate should they be? Another office? Another building? Another department altogether?

It is unlikely that there is a universal correct answer, although the authors would argue that the predominant category of maintenance is a key driver

—if this is, in the main, corrective, perfective or preventive maintenance then a separate team is probably most appropriate; if adaptive then collocation would be preferable.

The second issue is that of how to cope with a workload that is characterised by fluctuating resource requirements and (possibly) frequent requests for emergency action. One answer would be to allow the staff levels to fluctuate with the demand, but this all happens over very short time-scales and in practice that means taking people off other work and accepting the attendant problems.

The ideal solution would be to smooth out the fluctuations in the first place, by more detailed product-specific planning and by improvements in the areas of priority list control and release control that were referred to earlier.

Staff recruitment and motivation

Many people view maintenance as an unglamorous activity, and this attitude can make it difficult to recruit and motivate staff towards it. There appears to be no single reason for this, but for example:

● The very word 'maintenance' carries connotations of a less intellectual activity than 'design'.

● Where development and maintenance are separately organised, the developers may, understandably, be reluctant to admit that their creation requires so much effort to change, and may try to call into question the competence of the maintenance team rather than the quality of the program. (And sometimes, of course, they will be right!)

● Successful development will be publicised as an achievement. Successful maintenance will not.

The user viewpoint

The maintainers and end users of a system may have quite different views of the system's performance, and we have argued here that system performance indicators should include measures that are directly meaningful to the user. One example is the length of time taken to correct an error. For the maintainers, this is the elapsed time between receiving the problem report and successfully testing a modified version of the system. For the user it is the elapsed time between the initial perception of the problem and the successful installation of the new release.

Figure 7.2 shows a very simple network of maintenance functions. A user request may have to go through several of these functions before being attended to. Each individual function may respond quickly but the overall

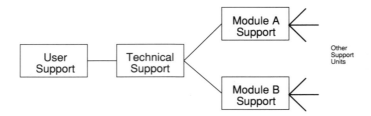

Figure 7.2   The chain of support for a single product

user view may be poor. In practice the facts that there are several versions of most products and most teams support more than one product complicate the network. The important point is to know what the network is and to be in a position to manage maintenance from the user's viewpoint.

Another aspect of user perception is the response to requests for relatively small adaptions to the system: in a DP system, for example, a small change in the format or content of a printed report. Although not a difficult change, it may well have to bide its time in the priority list before being attended to, and understandably the user may feel aggrieved as a result. Several authors (e.g. [Fos89]), in commenting on this problem, have shown how a system centred around a data-base management system (DBMS) allows the users themselves to develop their own reports once a suitable query language is made available to them, thus freeing the regular maintainers from that part of the workload.

7.5   THE SOFTWARE CONFIGURATION

The configuration of a product is the complete set of items associated with that product, including lists, source code, design documentation, build tools, test cases, etc. The process of controlling these items so that they are available when they are needed is known as *configuration management* (CM). Although relevant and important at all stages in software development, CM is dealt with in this chapter as it is, arguably, the most fundamental technical requirement for effective maintenance.

For many products, there is little need to treat hardware as part of the configuration. For example, in the case of DP programs running on a mainframe the configuration management of the mainframe itself is likely to be regarded as a separate task, with hopefully little impact on the CM of the individual products. To put it another way, the hardware is regarded as part of the product's environment, rather than as part of the product itself.

For embedded software products, however, the hardware within which they run is likely to be rather specialised and it is likely that there will be other hardware items, such as test equipment and diagnostic aids, without whose presence the main software cannot effectively be managed. Here, it is usually more convenient to regard the hardware as another component of a single configuration.

The degree of formality applied to configuration management will vary with the size and status of the project to which it is applied. At the lowest level, it will all be in the head of the single individual undertaking a casual and quick development; at the highest, it will be an elaborate scheme supported by formal manuals, and it will be a strong concern of the project management.

The components of configuration management may be separated out as follows [Kha75]:

- Configuration identification.

- Change control.

- Configuration auditing.

- Configuration status accounting.

Configuration identification

Configuration identification is the process of ensuring that all items of a configuration are discovered and uniquely identified, and that the identification includes means of distinguishing between different versions of the same item. It also provides the means for recording changes between versions of an item.

In the planning period, configuration identification is responsible for laying down the deliverables that will result from the project; in other words, it is used to describe what will happen, as well as to record what has happened.

There is a need in planning the method of configuration identification to decide whether variants of the product—versions running in parallel rather than in series with other versions—will be supported. It is necessary to avoid the temptation to take a 'decision' that they will not be required; the true decision will be taken by the reality of operational circumstances, where cost factors predominate and tidiness may have to come second.

Change control

When changes are made to items in the configuration, there has to be (or should be) a set of rules governing how they are instigated, evaluated, approved and implemented. These rules and procedures are collectively known as the change control mechanism.

Configuration auditing

A configuration audit is a periodic check to ensure the correct operation of the configuration identification and change control functions, and to ensure that the configuration as it exists reflects accurately the requirements and plans.

Since the configuration is the tangible embodiment of the entire project, the importance of this type of audit needs little emphasis.

Configuration status accounting

Configuration status accounting is concerned with the collation and presentation of the information from the other three components. In other words, it is the expression of the various states in the life of a product that can be referenced by anyone wanting to read the history of the project.

7.6   MAINTENANCE IN OPERATION

Although each of the four maintenance categories described above has its own characteristics, they have in common the fact that each consists of successive changes applied to pieces of software. In this section, the mechanics of implementing changes are briefly discussed, with a view to establishing and enumerating the components of the modification cycle.

The version of the modification cycle that is presented here is more elaborate than those found so far in the literature, probably because of the tendency of the literature to concentrate on DP applications, and thus to treat as relatively insignificant those aspects which are easier (cheaper) to perform in that environment. Those phases which, in the experience of the authors, have to be addressed are:

- Change request.

- Request evaluation.

- Design.

- Release Control.

- Build.

- Test.

- Distribution.

Each of these can be expanded in turn, as follows.

Change request

In this phase, a need or desire for a change first exists, and may then be perceived. Then, if its effect is sufficiently important, it may be notified. This gives rise to the three components:

- *Existence of need.* It has not been noticed yet, but something somewhere could be improved. There is much research interest in this area, mainly directed towards predicting from intrinsic program characteristics how many errors may be expected, as well as various other useful statistics.

- *Perception of need.* Something has been noticed, but not yet reported to the 'proper authority'. In an ideal situation, this phase is passed through very quickly; but if it is not (perhaps because the reporting procedure is difficult to penetrate) the effects on user satisfaction may be significant. The ways in which needs come to be perceived may also be worthy of study, since that could lead to useful techniques of anticipation for the maintenance team.

- *Notification of need.* Contact is made with the proper authority and the report is logged, for instance, through the submission of a request for change. The interest here is in the amount of detail that can usefully be communicated and in the best medium to use for the communication. Collection of data on where faults are found (and when they were introduced in the first place) is useful both to recreate (and subsequently fix) the fault and as data for future planning.

Request evaluation

In this phase, the benefit of the proposed change is balanced against the likely implementation cost, and the request is queued according to its resulting priority [Fos89]. Not all change proposals will require action: they may be cleared directly (e.g. if the problem is simply one of the user not operating the system correctly).

The components of this phase are :

- *Benefit assessment.* The expression of what will be gained from implementing the change. Ideally this will be presented in direct financial terms, but there are many possible aspects of benefit that cannot readily be so expressed.

- *Cost assessment.* How much the implementation of the change is expected to cost. When all factors are taken into account, this can be a very non-trivial calculation. For instance, loss of credibility is a very real cost that has to be balanced against more direct measures such as loss of revenue.

- *Priority assignment.* Based on the above two elements, a priority level is associated with the change proposal. If the benefit and cost can be expressed financially, then the priority level is merely the difference between the two (negative priority corresponding to 'not worth it'); otherwise the process can be difficult, subjective and time-consuming.

- *Priority list control.* The prioritised requests must be held in some convenient manner, so that subsequent maintenance effort can be directed where it is most cost-effective. The manner of achieving this has relevance also to release control.

(Re)Design

The components of this phase are very much the same as the components of the initial development part of the whole lifecycle, but with some augmentation:

- *Requirements evaluation.* This will be the most careful scrutiny yet of the change request.

- *Fault reproduction.* If the request is for a correction in the behaviour of the software, it is usually necessary to find a way of reproducing the problem at will. This permits diagnosis to occur (assuming that the reported symptoms were not in themselves sufficient to enable the error to be tracked down), and also provides a valuable confidence test: it should be impossible to reproduce the fault on the modified systems, using the same method.

- *Specification.* The change is described in behavioural terms.

- *Fault location.* For corrective maintenance again, the offending piece or pieces of code must be identified. Particularly for real-time and embedded systems, elaborate procedures and special equipment may be required.

- *Detailed design.* The actual code changes required are designed and recorded.

- *Design review.* An inspection of the design against the requirements and specification, to ensure that the requirements are met and no new errors are being generated.

Release control

This phase is concerned with the decision to create a new version of the software, incorporating some or all of the changes that are available. It receives scant attention in the literature (presumably because in many situations it is a simple process), but particularly when test and distribution costs are high it can merit significant attention. The components, which are heavily inter-related, are:

- *Release timing control.* This addresses the question of exactly when a new release of the software should be made. The main factors to balance against each other are: (a) the longer it's left, the more changes can be incorporated and so the greater the value, but (b) the sooner it's done, the greater are the total benefits from the changes that it does contain.

- *Release content control.* The decision as to which of the changes that are (or are expected to be) available should actually be included in a particular release. The default option, of course, is 'all of them', but there may be several reasons why some would be best delayed until future releases and these need to be evaluated and understood.

It is worth noting the desirability of predicting releases well before they happen, and for this reason there is interaction between the components of this phase and the change priority list referred to above (under request evaluation).

Build

In this phase, the code changes are applied to the source and the result is compiled to produce the new version of the software. As with release control, it will in many situations be a simple enough process; but as system complexity increases it becomes possible to identify at least the following components:

- *Parent version preparation.* The steps required to ensure that the source code and documentation which will be modified are indeed the intended versions.

- *Edit and review.* Entering the changes, and ensuring that errors are not introduced in that process.

- *Module construction.* The compilation and linkage process, together with any other associated items such as checksum generation, etc. Here, 'module' means any subcomponent of the system which can, at least in principle, be tested independently of the rest (for example, by enclosing it in a test harness which mimics the stimuli/response patterns of the target environment).

- *Integration.* Combining the individual modules to create the complete system.

- *Archiving.* The safe preservation of the modified code and documentation.

Test

The range of tests that may be applied to a newly generated piece of software is extremely wide—the main issues and techniques were introduced in the previous chapter. However, it may be observed that in general, the testing of change that has been made to a piece of software will fall into three categories:

- *Confidence testing.* The main intended effect of the change is demonstrated.

- *Localised testing.* A check is made to see that all expected effects of the change are indeed observed. If the change is sufficiently small, it may well be possible to ensure during this test that all modified code is executed—something that is rarely possible for a system as a whole.

- *Non-localised testing.* The operation of the system as a whole is checked, in an attempt to reveal any unintended side-effects of the changes.

Each of these varieties of test may take many forms, and each may be applied to the fully constructed system or to any component module before integration.

Distribution

The components of the distribution phase vary widely according to the application, but a basic list of components would be:

- *Presentation.* The software will be sent out as a package, and the form and content of the package must be designed and its accuracy checked.

- *Replication.* Copies must be produced for every site where the software is installed. This is easy enough in many cases, but it can be expensive for embedded systems, where the software must be placed in ROM and very many copies may have to be made. It may also be expensive where a system is customised: that is, where different sites require different variants to be produced from a master generic.

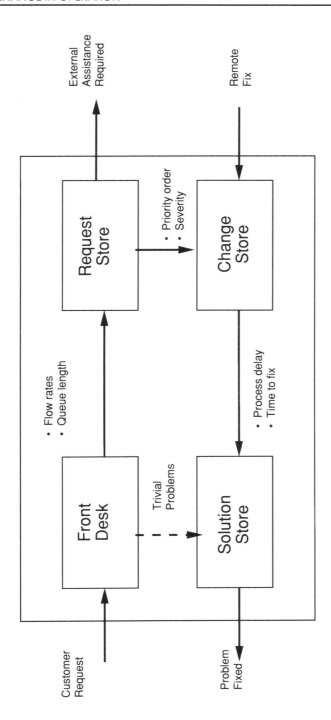

Figure 7.3   The functions and measures inside the support unit

- *Delivery.* In many cases this is a simple enough task, but the embedded systems again provide a counter-example. Small telephone exchanges are usually ROM-based embedded systems, and the delivery of a new release involves visits to sites in Scotland, Wales, Cornwall, the Orkneys, the Hebrides and the Shetlands—and that's just for the UK version!

- *Installation.* The new copy of the software must be installed and its operation verified, and site records must be maintained. Again, costs can vary widely.

Figure 7.3. shows how the various activities considered in this Section fit together. The maintenance team can be considered to be performing a linked set of functions, dealing first with request handling (reception and evaluation), then with design and test, then build and, finally, release. The model represented in the figure is a useful one in two ways. First, it clearly differentiates some of the key activities within a maintenance team and provides a basis for assigning team roles (in a small team one person may take on several roles, in a large team several people may share one role).

The second use of this model of the maintenance team is that it clarifies the types of measures that can be applied to gauge the maintenance process. Some measures (such as number of requests for change per unit time) are fairly obvious and would apply to any maintenance team, others (for instance, requests for change actioned per release) may be useful for specifc products. In either case, once the process is sensibly measured, it can be controlled and improved.

One final issue on maintenance in action concerns the use of tools in maintenance. The simple point is that they are essential in any significant project and that they come in too wide a variety to do them justice in this text. Useful tools for the maintainer range from straightforward compilers, linkers, etc. (which often provide cross reference functions) through configuration management and build systems through to sophisticated restructuring and re-engineering aids.

7.7   IMPROVING MAINTENANCE

The focus of this chapter so far has been on what the key issues are in maintaining a software system. To complete the treatment of the topic we now consider three of the areas in which there is significant promise that existing maintenance problems could be eased. These are:

- *Reverse engineering.* A means of improving the current practice of software maintenance.

- *Measurement.* A means of establishing a deeper understanding of the maintenance process and determining through objective data what can best be done.

● *Design for maintenance.* Attempting to lessen the future maintenance through prevention at the design stage (as opposed to cure after delivery).

Reverse engineering

Software documentation should be produced as a by-product of the development process and handed over as a complete package, along with the source code, to the team that will maintain the program. However, this is rarely the situation in practice. Most software projects reach completion without useful documentation for the people that have to maintain it.

The maintenance programmer has, therefore, to reconstruct the program documentation from the code in order to achieve an appropriate understanding of how the system works. It will not in general be possible to reconstruct all (or even any) of the transformations that occurred between the original requirements and the final code. Nonetheless much can be gleaned from a study of the code. The benefits of this approach can be greatly enhanced by a system of documentation which allows such discoveries to be recorded quickly and easily, so that the recording process becomes simply a spin-off of the maintenance process and does not unduly disturb the engineer's train of thought.

There have been a number of studies into the process of understanding and documenting existing programs [War89] but they have, in general, concentrated on fairly small programs. In such cases it is possible to understand the operation of the whole program within reasonable limits of time and effort. The maintenance engineer who is faced with a large program (which is, perhaps, the area of most concern) is not in a position to consider the whole program but must instead identify just those portions which are immediately relevant and concentrate on those.

In essence this is 'reverse engineering': the ability to reconstruct the logical shape of software from source code. This exercise is a crucial part of understanding what the system does and hence a vital precursor to maintaining that code, in much the same way that, in medicine, anatomy enables surgery. Tools to support reverse engineering have started to become commercially available over the last few years, predominantly in support of COBOL programmes. There is increasing interest in reverse engineering as it is rapidly moving towards being an established technique in some areas, notably data processing systems.

Measurement

In order to perform maintenance more effectively, it is essential to measure the process. At present there is no objective means of assessing the effects of the various design approaches on maintenance, although there are useful measures that can be made on maintained software. For instance, statistics on time taken to fix an error can, when related back to where the fault report originated (e.g. missing requirement, coding error), provide a measure of maintainability on the original techniques employed.

Although work has been carried out in this area, there is little useful data available. Almost all of the literature published to date has concentrated on either data processing or scientific programming, much of the data is ten years old and is based on projects (mostly military) carried out in the US.

The ultimate goal of measurement is the establishment of links between the maintainability of a piece of software and the design practices that were used to produce it. In view of the high proportion of time and money that software maintenance consumes, this would be a most telling measure of the effectiveness of the various design approaches described in Chapter 5.

Design for maintainability

In the absence of the above data, it is nonetheless important that maintainability is considered from the very outset of the software development process. The adoption of quality management procedures such as ISO 9000 (explained in the next chapters) acknowledges the need for traceability throughout the development lifecycle and the need for controlled and documented design procedures.

Technically, the loop is now closed—the future of maintenance points back to earlier phases of the development process and their correlation with one of the key non-functional requirements: maintainability.

There is little doubt that management practice will play an important part in this area and the next chapters concentrate on that role. The final part of this chapter is a brief checklist for the maintainer.

7.8   A MAINTENANCE CHECKLIST

Given the broad scope of activities in the maintenance phase, all of the checklists in this book are relevant here. The points below concentrate on some of the issues highlighted in this chapter—product release, configuration management, etc. The checklist below is structured into five main sections.

The system

- What machines, operating systems and languages are involved?
  (It is essential to have a clear picture of the basic equipment needed to recreate all instances of a released system.)

- Is the system a one-off or will there be many installations?
  (Replication and delivery to many sites, often with different documentation and build requirements, needs to be planned for.)

- What is the expected life of the system?
  (There are different considerations, plans and priorities in maintaining
  a system for one year as opposed to 20 years; refer to the 'deathcycle'
  section of Chapter 3 for more detail.)

The software

- How big is the program?
  (Even an approximate number of lines of code is useful—a rule of thumb
  is that one person can maintain 17kloc per annum.)

- How was the system designed?
  (The method used to create the software can be useful in understanding
  its structure and, hence, ease its maintenance.)

- Is any component of the software supplied by a third party?
  (Apart from the language(s) used, built-in components may imply dependence in the maintenance network.)

The maintenance organisation

- How and in what form is documentation kept?
  (Is it up to date? on-line? relevant to the code being maintained? Design
  documentation is often less used in maintenance than in cross reference
  catalogues, etc.)

- Where do the responsibilities for maintenance lie?
  (Who handles enquiries, first line and second line support.)

- Does a fault reporting scheme exist?
  (There should be a mechanism for recording and dealing with requests
  for change. This is a basic requirements and provides a first point of reference for measuring the process.)

- Do any statements exist on the expected annual cost of maintenance?
  (An understanding of the real costs of maintenance are vital in phasing
  the product life—see Chapter 3 on the 'deathcycle'.)

Configuration management

- Can all of the versions and variants of the system be retrieved and built? (Often there are many similar but not identical products maintained in the same area.)

- Are procedures for CM defined? (Project files, source libraries, compatability lists, release notes, etc. all need to be controlled. There must be procedures for change.)

- What recovery procedures are in place? (If there was a fire in the department, how serious would it be—loss of a day's work, a week's, or everything?)

7.9   SUMMARY

Given the ever-increasing importance of software in the IT industry and the high proportion of resources consumed in software maintenance, this is likely to be an area of growing concern through the 1990s. This chapter has explained the key issues and techniques required to effectively tackle an important but often neglected area.

The main message has been that maintenance is not a simple matter of correcting errors after software is released. It is an ongoing process of keeping software in tune with user requirements and the maintenance process has to be organised to cope with changes in function, environment and the like, as well as reported faults.

The implications of this are significant. First, it is vital to clearly understand the types of maintenance required and the phases that a maintained software system passes through. The types described here are:

- Corrective maintenance (repair maintenance).

- Adaptive maintenance (e.g. to cope with a new operating system).

- Perfective maintenance (maintenance to optimise performance, etc.).

- Preventative maintenance (to increase robustness).

The phases are:

- *Enhancement,* in which the specification of the product undergoes considerable alteration. (This phase is recognisable from its tendency to emit 'major new releases'.)

- *Maturity,* in which the specification remains relatively stable and the main activity (if any) is corrective maintenance.

- *Obsolescence*, in which the product remains available and in use, but the ability to alter it has been lost.

- *Termination*, in which the product may still be in use, but all control has been abandoned.

Second, it important to control the modification cycle of a system in maintenance. Much of the technical work carried out by the maintainer has been covered in the previous chapters on design and testing. There are, however, extra constraints on the maintainer imposed by the existing body of software that must continue to operate without change as new features are added and known errors are fixed.

7.10   REFERENCES

[Can72] Canning, R. (1972) That maintenance iceberg, *EDP Analyzer* **10.10** pp 1–14.

[Fos89] Foster, J.R. (1989) Priority control in software maintenance, *Proc. 7th Int. Conf. on Software for Telecomms Switching Systems* pp163–167.

[GEC86] General Electric Company (1986) *Software Engineering Handbook* (McGraw-Hill).

[KI84] Kling, R. and Iacono, S. (1984) The control of information systems developments after implementation, *CACM* **27.12** pp1218–1226.

[LS80] Leintz, B.P. and Swanson, E.B. (1980) *Software Maintenance Management* (Addison-Wesley).

[Swa76] Swanson, E.B. (1976) The dimensions of maintenance, *Proc. 2nd Int. Conf. on Software Engineering* pp 493–497.

[War89] Warden, R.H. Software re-engineering, a practical approach, *Proc. Conf. on Software Tools* pp 423–434.

[Kha75] Khan, Z. (1975) How to tackle the systems maintenance dilemma *Canadian Datasystems* pp 30–32.

8

A History of Quality

Quality is optional, you don't have to survive
Philip Crosby

In the previous chapters we have discussed the best technical practices throughout the software lifecycle. In this chapter we will provide a brief outline of the contents and history of quality management covering both Total Quality Management (TQM) and Quality Management System (QMS) techniques in use at present. The object of this chapter is to give a background to how quality systems have developed and how they can be applied to software. Unfortunately, most of the examples are from the hardware industries as there is less practical experience in software quality than hardware. Nonetheless the process of software production is becoming increasingly well understood with ISO 9000 and TQM being the state of the art.

In the next chapter we will discuss the operational aspects of quality management systems based on ISO 9000. The last chapter consists of predictions of where we are going in software quality.

8.1 TOTAL QUALITY MANAGEMENT (TQM)

TQM is the method of quality improvement used originally by the Japanese. It can be argued that the use of TQM techniques is one of the main reasons for the commercial success of Japan in the last forty years. TQM was not invented in Japan but found fertile ground there for its development and growth. It was imported from the USA after the Second World War by Dr W. Edwards Deming and Dr Joseph Juran. Both of these men found their way to Japan after their work had been rejected by the leading companies in their own country. Dr Deming was a Doctor of Physics working for the the US government. He was sent to Japan by the US army to help with its census and was asked to address the Japanese Union of Scientists and

Engineers (JUSE). His method was based on a statistical approach to sampling techniques but the main theme is a systematic and rigorous approach to quality. Dr Juran arrived in Japan in 1954 with his basic messages of focusing on quality rather than cost and of attaining the quality breakthrough. His ideas have been under constant development in Japan ever since.

Japan has now produced its own gurus. One of the best known is Professor Ishikawa who pioneered quality circles and the Ishikawa diagram, also known as the fish bone diagram. Another well known name from Japan is Dr Genichi Taguchi whose method calls for the quality and reliability of a product to be built in at the design stage, stressing that you cannot paint on the quality after you have produced the product. Almost all the work undertaken by the above gurus was hardware or service based but many of the principles can be applied to the software industry.

The basis of TQM is a quality-centred production model. This contrasts with the cost-centred model shown in Figure 8.1 which is the traditional method used for production in the West. The cost-centred model with its emphasis on costs can achieve short-term returns. It takes the short-term view of quality cost. This approach was challenged by Dr Deming who argued that the primary focus should be on quality.

The quality-centred model, shown in Figure 8.2, reflects a very different approach. In this case the focus is on continual quality improvement. This model, with its emphasis on quality rather than cost, takes a longer-term view relying on an improvement in quality to produce the cost reductions.

Figure 8.1   A cost centred model

Figure 8.2 A quality centred model

In operation, this model aims to close the quality loop (repeat the process) and hence generate continual quality improvement.

The Japanese took to this system in the 1950s after Deming persuaded the Japanese Union of Scientists and Engineers to take the quality-centred approach. He also ensured the customer is brought into the process and by creating a link between the manufacturers and suppliers, continuous quality improvement is ensured. This allowed the Japanese to develop the JIT (Just in Time) technique. The basics of this system are that you trust your supplier's product ability to deliver quality products on time and hence do not need to keep contingency stocks.

Dr Juran added the concept of quality breakthrough. This basically means you should not only reduce quality cost but control variation around the norm. Figure 8.3 shows a reduction in quality cost and a reduction of variation about the mean. The breakthrough is by the reduction in chronic quality cost such as rework, etc.

Juran found that 90% of all quality problems were caused by the management and not the workers. Hence, most benefits come from training managers not only in their job but in people management and statistical techniques. The object is to make the manager a facilitator rather than a dictator. This is one of the underlying principals of the TQM approach to quality.

The application of TQM is best demonstrated by the Japanese car industry. Cars have been manufactured in Japan since the 1920s, but export only took off in the 1960s. The method used to gain pre-eminence in car production is the same one applied to the motorcycle industry TV, radio, ship building, etc. First find (or invent in the case of the Walkman) a market niche. In Figure 8.4 the niche is between Ford and General Motors. You then supply your product in the same price range but to a better specification than your competition. In the case of this car, supply a heater and radio

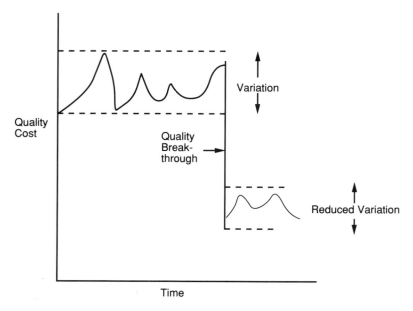

Figure 8.3   A quality breakthrough graph

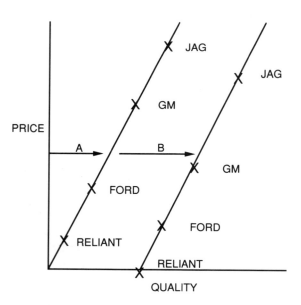

Figure 8.4   Quality perceptions graph

as standard when your competitors supply these items as optional extras. This is point A in Figure 8.4.

You then improve the quality of your product by using the quality-centred approach (Figure 8.2) and keep the price the same by using the quality control approach to production. This is point B in Figure 8.4. Your competition cannot compete on quality and hence must reduce its profit margins to compete. By this process the customer's perception of your product is improved and you move up the perception graph. You are now perceived as better than GM but not yet as good as Jaguar.

At the same time the customer's overall perception of the Japanese car improves against its competition and its market share increases. This drives the rest of your opposition down the perception line on the price–quality graph while maintaining your own position.

We have seen the first companies go to the wall, e.g. Bond and Reliant (Skoda and Lada will follow when their subsidy is removed unless they change their product quality).

The way this process is controlled is by accurate knowledge of customer requirements and control of the production process to improve quality and hence reduce cost. Car manufacturers in the west have now realised the key role of quality and are now applying TQM techniques to their manufacturing.

In the USA the Harley Davidson Motorcycle Company realised this just in time and put in place a quality improvement program. The British motorcycle companies were not quick enough—neither were most of our TV, radio, shipbuilding and hi-fi industries.

This may not seem at first sight to have much relevance to the software industry but the first person to find the metrics that measure process control will be able to apply the same techniques to software. Will the European software industry be any different from the other industries that have gone to the wall?

The previous section has been a very basic introduction to some TQM principles. There are many good reference books on this subject, some listed in the bibliography. The heart of a total quality management programme is

- Management training.

- Techniques training for all (Pareto analysis, etc.).

- Corporate culture development.

A cornerstone of TQM is to place the responsibility for quality in the hands of the people that can control it. This may mean moving the responsiblity for quality to the operative at a machine. But with this responsibility comes accountablity and authority, for which training is required. Section 8.2 outlines how the factory system of the industrial revolution took responsibility away from the operative, with its target of quantity rather than quality. TQM is attempting to redress the balance and foster pride in a job well done.

The other current major quality technique is the use of quality management systems.

8.2   QUALITY MANAGEMENT SYSTEMS

The history of quality management systems can be traced back as far as the Pharaohs in Egypt, when funerary goods had to be approved by the Superintendent of the Necropolis and bear his mark.

The roots of modern quality standards stem from the Industrial Revolution. In the UK the revolution was fuelled by a desire to supply cheap goods to the ever-expanding Empire.

The emphasis on quality over quantity came from the USA where the requirements of the military and settlers in the expanding west demanded guns with interchangeable parts. This led to what was known as the American system of manufacture, a method of high-precision mass production. Until this time, guns were handmade on a one-off basis and hence replacement parts were also handmade by highly skilled and experienced gunsmiths. There was at this time a shortage of these skills in the USA.

The American system of manufacture was developed using as its base automatic control with an unskilled immigrant workforce from Europe employed as machine loaders and watchers. These machines had to be set up and their adjustment monitored by highly skilled tradesmen. This can be considered as quality inspection throughout the process. This form of mass production was also responsible for the introduction of productivity measurement, time and motion studies and the division of the labour force into management, skilled tradesmen and unskilled labourers.

The skilled tradesmen were responsible for the inspection and hence quality of the production process. As the size of companies increased and the complexity of the goods produced also increased, this inspection process was passed from one tradesman to the next down the manufacturing line.

The next step was the introduction of inspectors who were independent of the manufacturing operation who would inspect the goods and return any that were defective for rectification.

The first successful attempt to document and standardise this process was an American military specification MIL-Q-9858.A in 1963.

The development of standards then followed the diagram shown in Figure 8.5. The instruments of change are illustrated for clarification. NATO set up the Allied Quality Assurance Publication (AQAP) as a derivative of the US MIL standard. The UK, despite being a member of NATO, set up its own defence standard DEF.STAN 05/21, 05/24, and 05/29 again in a similar format to both AQAP and US MIL standards.

The need for a commercial industry standard for quality assurance in the UK was met by the British Standards Institute, who produced BS 5750 in 1979.

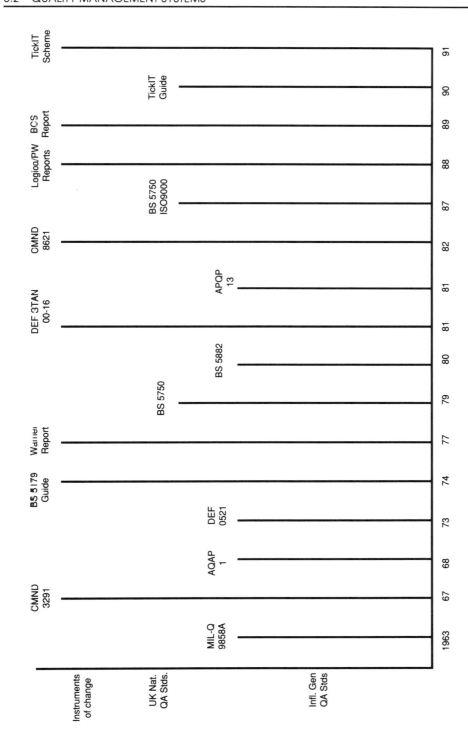

Figure 8.5   Developments in quality assurance over the last 30 years

Standards body	Quality management and quality assurance standards guidelines for selection and use	Quality systems model for quality assurance in design/development, production, installation, and servicing	Quality systems model for quality assurance in production and installation	Quality systems model for quality assurance in final inspection and test	Quality management and quality system element guidelines
ISO	ISO 9000 1987	ISO 9001 1987	ISO 9002 1987	ISO 9003 1987	ISO 9004 1987
Austrailia	AS 3900	AS 3901	AS 3902	AS 3903	AS 3904
Belguim	NBN X 50-002-1	NBN X 50-003	NBN X 50-004	NBN X 50-005	NBN X 50-002-2
Canada	-	-	-	-	CSA Q420-87
European Community	EN 29000 1987	EN 29001-1987	EN 29002-1987	EN 29003 1987	EN 29004-1987
India	ISS 10201 Part 2	IS 10201 Part 4	IS 10201 Part 5	IS 10201 Part 6	IS 10201 Part 3
South Africa	SABS 0157: Part 0	SABS 0157: Part 1	SABS 0157: Part II	SABS 0157: Part III	SABS 0157: Part IV
Spain	UNE 66 900	UNE 66 901	UNE 66 902	UNE 66 903	UNE 66 904
Switerland	SN-ISO 9000	SN-ISO 9001	SN-ISO 9002	SN-ISO 9003	SN-ISO 9004
USA	ANSI/ASQC Q90-1987	ANSI/ASQC Q91-1987	ANSI/ASQC Q92-1987	ANSI/ASQC Q93-1987	ANSI/ASQC Q94-1987
USSR	-	40.9001-88	40 9002-88	-	-
West German	DIN ISO 9000	DIN ISO 9001	DIN ISO 9002	DIN ISO 9003	DIN ISO 9004

Figure 8.6   Quality systems world wide

This was further refined until 1987 when the International Standards Organisation produced ISO 9000 which was based on BS 5750.

The ISO 9000 consists of four parts: ISO 9001, 9002, 9003, 9004:

ISO 9000.   Quality Management and Quality Assurance Standards—Guidelines for Selection and Use.

ISO 9001.   Quality Systems—Model for Quality Assurance in Design/Development, Production, Installation and Servicing.

ISO 9002.   Quality Systems—Model for Quality Assurance in Production and Installation.

ISO 9003.   Quality Systems—Model for Quality Assurance in Final Inspection and Test.

ISO 9004.   Quality Management and Quality System Elements—Guidelines.

The ISO 9000 standards have been adopted by the national standards systems of most manufacturing countries worldwide (Figure 8.6). In the European Community it is known as Euronorme EN29000-1987.

Basically ISO 9000 is all about documenting and standardising the process just as the gunsmiths in the USA did. It represents the current best practice in management and control when applied to software production.

We, in the software industry, are at the same stage the gun manufacturers of the USA were in before industrialisation—a few gurus who make very good systems and the rest who often deliver poor quality software late. Will history repeat itself? It looks very much like it with the quest for metrics, formal methods, etc. We are now at the stage of injecting quality into software and are attempting to move to quality assurance. This is where the Quality Management Systems come into their own. Before describing ISO 9000 in detail, we will attempt to answer some common questions and outline the benefits.

8.3   A BRIEF GUIDE TO THE ISO 9000 QUALITY SYSTEMS

Some common questions about ISO 9000 answered

(a) What is ISO 9000?
ISO 9000 is concerned with the quality assurance of functional organisation capabilities.

(b) Why is it needed?
There must be a basic plan for quality. It does not just happen. This is just one way of continuously meeting the requirements and expectations of customers.

(c) What is a quality plan?

A document setting out the specific quality practices resources and activities relevant to a particular product, service contract or project.

(d) What is quality assurance?

The assurance to the customer that effective procedures exist to ensure all requirements of the design will be met and the product resulting from the total engineering design will be satisfactory. This is an offical definition. A better one is: quality assurance is the business of ensuring that good software is not the result of good luck but the reward for good management practice.

(e) Who does it affect and what are their responsibilities?

Anyone associated with planning, sales, training, supply, manufacture, inspection, testing, customer services, engineering, field service; in short, almost everyone. The responsibilities of the customer, people involved in the process and the supplier are shown in Figure 8.7 [ISO91].

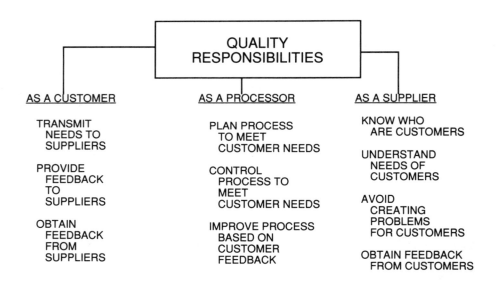

Figure 8.7 Quality responsibilities (after Juran)

(f) What does ISO 9000 require?

The following pages outline the different requirements which, if complied with, will mean the company is operating a good management system.

What are the benefits for the customer?

(a) A known level of quality that is defined and can be measured.

(b) A level of service that has been and continues to be independently audited.

(c) A performance that should continue to improve.

(d) A means of choosing between competitive offerings.

(e) Confidence in the services provided.

What are the benefits for the company?

(a) Improved quality through:
   (1) Increased staff awareness, and
   (2) Consistency of products and services.

(b) Employees understand their role and objectives by having a documented management system.

(c) Increased morale, by developing a sense of pride in achieving goals and providing customer satisfaction.

(d) Improved productivity and cost savings making the company more competitive.

(e) An efficient management system.

The parts of ISO 9001

The ISO 9001 document is a generic model for a quality management system. The same document can be used to build a quality system in almost any product or service. To make ISO 9001 applicable to the software industry supporting documentation has been produced by the International Standards Organisation. The Guidelines for the application of ISO 9001 to the development, supply and maintenance of software [ISO91] have been given the confusing number of ISO9000-3 (note the dash). All 20 parts of ISO 9001 still apply, but to help the understanding of each section a short guide with comments is included.

Requirement 1. Management responsibility/quality policy

There must be a definite programme for quality. The policy must be communicated and understood throughout the company. Management must regularly review the whole quality system to ensure its continued effectiveness and conformance to ISO 9000. There must be effective management for quality with all responsibilities clearly defined in writing and sufficient resources to do the job.

- We must have management,… with authority,… and defined responsibility.
- Obvious really! 'Just good management'.

Requirement 2. Quality system

All the systems that directly or indirectly affect the quality of our product and services must be documented. The documentation must be practical, current, complete and effectively controlled. It must also correspond to what really happens.

- It is essential that we all know what we are supposed to do.
- Documentation is the foundation of all good working practices.

Requirement 3. Contract review

We must ensure that:

(a) We know what customer requirements are.

(b) Those requirements are documented and reviewed.

(c) Any changes to requirements are resolved.

(d) We are able to meet requirements.

(e) We have customer agreement.

- Contracts and orders must be reviewed to ensure we continue to meet them.
- Customers must receive the products and services specified.

Requirement 4. Design control

This requirement aims to ensure the finished design of products or services meets those needs specified by the customer.

- Design is the foundation of quality. Chapters 4 and 5 stress the need to plan and review system structure and function at an early stage.

Requirement 5. Document control

People need to know what they are required to do. Therefore, working practices must be documented, up to date, controlled and readily available. Obsolete documents should be removed promptly from use.

- Are we up to date? Are we all using the same documentation?
- A vital part of configuration management.

Requirement 6. Purchasing

Materials, parts, and services that are bought from suppliers must be fit for purpose, meet our quality requirements, and be controlled. Purchase specifications must be clearly written so that a supplier knows where he stands and knows exactly what is wanted.

- The aim is to purchase only goods and services that are of the appropriate quality. This requirement also includes vendor appraisal and assessment of subcontractors.

Requirement 7. Purchaser supplied product

Customers may supply materials to be used on their jobs. Such materials must be securely stored and methods used to prevent deterioration or loss.

- Look after your own and other people's property.

Requirement 8. Product identification and traceability

At any time it is important to know what any item is; what it belongs to; at what stage it is; what stages it has already completed; what was used to build it; where did parts come from and who did what to it? Once an item has been built, it is important we know where it goes. Where appropriate, there must be forward and backward traceability.

- If an item goes wrong at any time, its history tells us what to do to prevent further failures. Large software systems have many components, it is essential to be able to put the right ones together.

Requirement 9. Process control

Production and installation must occur under controlled conditions. Employees must know what to do and what standards are required. Controls should exist to ensure that only good-quality products are provided. The operation may be complex; it might need special checks, additional instructions, special training and qualifications. Adequate work instructions, and standards to be met, should be written down to ensure work is done correctly with suitable tools, parts, methods, specifications, etc.

Consistent quality requires controlled processes. A work instruction is always required, if the absence of one would affect quality.

- Work instructions should be easily understood, practical, short, to the point,..., and used.

Requirement 10. Inspection and testing

Products must be inspected or verified, and pass the acceptance criteria when being received, worked on, and prior to dispatch. Any products not conforming to these standards must be segregated so that corrective action can be carried out. Records should be kept for inspection work done in each stage.

- Ensure that the final product meets all of the specifications. This is VV&T by another name (see Chapter 6).

Requirement 11. Inspection measuring and test equipment

Equipment used for checking or testing of a product must be capable of accurately performing those functions. It is also required that:

- All testing and measuring equipment is identified.

- Records show the frequency of calibration.

- Procedures for calibration exist and that calibration is traceable to recognised standards, e.g. BS 5781.

- Instructions exist on how to deal with products that have been checked using equipment which subsequently fails calibration.

- This is not as important in software development, but becomes more important in systems development.

Requirement 12. Inspection and test status

When any product moves through a process its status must be obvious. This can be achieved by using cards, labels, records, physical location or other suitable means. Only products which pass the required tests are to be used or dispatched and should indicate who carried out the checks at each stage.

- Distinguish between inspected and uninspected—good and bad. This is version control and just part of good configuration management.

Requirement 13. Control of non-conforming products

Even in the best systems things go wrong—the product doesn't conform— scrap is made. When this happens the product must be identified and seg- regated. Precise procedures must be established to rework the material to dispose as appropriate. Above all, defective material or products must not be allowed to become mixed with good products.

- Reducing scrap and the need for rework increases efficiency. Do we have scrap software (see Chapter 1)? We definitely have too much rework.

Requirement 14. Corrective action

All procedures, processes and products need to be monitored and reviewed to ensure constant delivery of quality. Any non-conformance to standards must be documented, analysed, the cause identified and corrective action taken to avoid a re-occurence.

- This is a constant process and involves everyone. Customer complaint handling is also part of this corrective action.

Requirement 15. Handling storage, packaging and delivery

Products must be handled carefully to prevent damage. They must be stored in secure controlled areas. All packaging must be to an adequate standard and therefore prevent damage or deterioration to products whilst in stor- age or delivery.

- Handle with care!

Requirement 16. Quality records

Quality records must be maintained so we can demonstrate our level of achievement against required standards and hence prove the effectiveness of the quality system. All records must be legible, easily retrieved, and methods must be employed to prevent deterioration or loss.

- Records are the proof of achievement and provide the trail for finding errors to enable the process to be improved. Examples of quality records are review follow-up action list, audit corrective action list. The importance of records is demonstrated in Chapter 9.

Requirement 17. Internal quality audits

The internal quality assurance auditors carry out impartial independent assessments and reviews to check whether processes and procedures are still pertinent, effective and meet requirements.

- Are we as good as we think we are?

Requirement 18. Training

For employees to perform tasks satisfactorily and meet the required standards, they must be shown the correct methods and techniques to use. Appropriate training must be provided and future needs identified. Records of this training and of any skills attained must be kept.

- You should document both on- and off-the-job training as well as experience. There should be a plan of any further training required.

Requirement 19. Servicing

Where servicing of equipment is a requirement, it must be well specified, carried out by adequately trained personnel and within agreed timescales.

- Servicing done well, on time, by adequately trained staff leads to happy satisfied customers.

Requirement 20. Statistical techniques

Checking or testing the acceptability of products and processes can be done on a sample basis, but the sample must be representative of the whole. Records must be maintained in order to identify trends and assist in forecasting.

- We do not yet have any universally accepted metrics that can be used to predict or quantify software. There are two main types of software development measurements, the product and process metrics. These should be collected within the project management system used for the development. The object is to produce accurate repeatable and accepted measures.

These 20 requirements explain what has to be brought under control to install a QMS to the ISO 9000 standard. We have been through the basics of TQM and ISO 9000. The installation of a quality improvement programme based upon either TQM or QMS techniques is too big a topic for this book. A good place to start with TQM is *Deming's 14 Points For Managers* [BDA86]. Assuring quality in software, practical experiences in attaining ISO 9001 [RSN90] will provide an insight into the implementation of ISO 9001 in the software field. Now for how TQM and ISO 9001are linked and fitted together.

8.4 THE LINK BETWEEN TQM AND QMS

How a QMS and TQM are linked depend upon your viewpoint. One simplistic viewpoint is that the QMS gives you control and discipline in your process and TQM builds constant quality improvement into your system. A widely accepted model [RSN90] is to draw the analogy with the clock spring mechanisms. TQM is the key which tensions the main spring. The QMS is pawl in the ratchet that hold the tension, or, putting it another way, TQM gives you the quality drive and the QMS holds the gains.

In the move from anarchy to quality as described in Chapter 1 we use the model:

● Say what you do.

● Do what you say.

● Be able to prove it.

All of these are QMS functions but the next stage is to improve the process. This is where the strength of TQM comes to the fore.

To enable the software industry to produce quality software we need both approaches to start with. You then build a hybrid of the two to suit your requirements. There are many people in the quality business who argue the advantage of QMS over TQM and vice versa. This is a pointless exercise. The Japanese, with 40 years experience of TQM are now taking on elements of ISO 9000 to enhance these systems. Whatever system you use the maxim 'Quality is optional, you don't have to survive' applies [Cro80].

A recent development in the quality field has been to drop the management from TQM and call it Total Quality (TQ). This has the advantage of helping to push the point that Quality is everybody's business, not just the concern of management. The time may now be right to use TQ to describe the process of the production of software. It can be considered to consist of three main areas of Financial Management, Project Management and Quality Management. The importance of these areas depend upon your point of view.

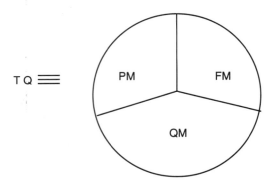

Figure 8.8   Viewpoint of quality

Total Quality is when you have all those areas under control and are constantly improving quality in all of the areas. Total Quality software will be delivered on time, to budget and meeting the customer's requirements first time and every time. This is not too much to ask from the customer's point of view. As an industry we are not there yet but we are getting better!

8.5   SUMMARY

In this chapter we have outlined the principles, parts and history of the quality management techniques available to the software industry. The benefits of a QMS together with its constituent parts (based on ISO 9000) are shown, as this is the most used QMS for software. The link between the TQM and the QMS approach, together with a simple model, has been proposed. The SEI method [SEI91] used in the USA is not included as its function is to measure the maturity of a company's software process. It is not a full quality management system.

In an attempt to link TQM and QMS systems together a simple analogy, the clock spring mechanism, has been proposed.

8.6   REFERENCES

[BDA86] British Deming Association (1986) *Deming's 14 Points For Managers* (2 Castle Street, Salisbury, Wiltshire SP11BB, UK).

[Cro80] Crosby, Philip B. (1980) *Quality is Free* (Mentor, New York).

[ISO91] ISO (1991) International Standard ISO 9000-3 Quality management and quality assurance standards part 3. Reference number ISO9000-3:1991(e).

[RSN90] Rigby, P.J., Stoddart A.G. and Norris, M.T. (1990) *British Telecommunications Engineering Journal* **8.1** p.244.

[SEI91] SEI Process Assessment, *IEEE Software* July 1991.

9

Quality Management Systems

Managing software engineers is like herding cats

Anon

9.1 INTRODUCTION

In the first chapter of this book we discussed why quality matters from a financial and safety point of view. One viewpoint of quality and quality management systems is as a means of closing the quality loop of the process (see Figure 9.1). We have described the overall software process

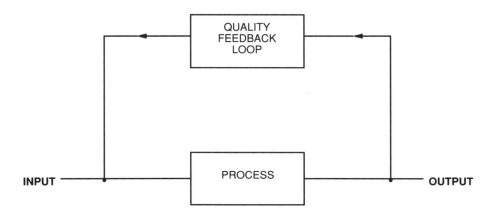

Figure 9.1 The quality feedback loop

and the elements within it. We now intend to close the quality loop by discussing:

1. A view of the process of managing a QMS.

2. A list of common pitfalls of installing and maintaining a QMS.

3. A checklist for implementing a QMS.

4. Where next with the software QMS?

The aim of this chapter is to try and clarify the operation of a quality system based on ISO 9000, to show how it functions and to list common pitfalls. A checklist for implementing a QMS is also included. The final section of this chapter outlines recent developments in software-specific quality management systems and looks at the legal aspect of software quality.

9.2 MANAGING A QMS

It cannot be stressed too much that quality is a people-management issue If the actions and reactions, of all staff, become quality driven then expensive failures and reworks can be drastically reduced or even eliminated. Too often quality is treated as a technical problem and technical fixes are applied which do not work. An effective quality management system is necessarily people-based. It needs to contain procedures and prescribed activities such as the technical issues covered in Chapters 4–7 but the necessary prerequisite is that people apply the available technology in a sensible way. From past experience the pitfalls of a QMS are usually people-related as shown in Section 9.3.

The starting point for any quality system is a clear management policy stating why the system exists. Any policy which puts assessment to ISO 9000 as its primary objective is not satisfactory. The policy must state the reasons for having a quality system in terms of the organisation's business. The QMS is, in effect, part of the corporate strategy.

An example of a quality policy is as follows:

The department will provide competitive products and services which fully meet the agreed requirements of our internal and external clients. Products and services will be delivered:

- to specification, first time
- on time, every time.

All staff are personally responsible for the quality of their own work and work done under their supervision.

All work done will be to the appropriate standards and will comply with the department's quality management system.

The quality management system will:
- satisfy the quality policy
- add value to the business
- comply with the requirements of ISO 9001.

Given a policy framed like this it is possible, easy even, to define the scope and content of a quality system to satisfy it.

Techniques and standards used in Quality Management Systems

Figure 9.2 [Cro90] contains many important features of a QMS. The main ones are explained below.

QA audits

QA audits [BSI89] examine all aspects of projects at the time of the audit. They should be conducted by people with considerable interpersonal skills and sensitivity. The audit report should add value to the auditees and line managers and hence should give a balanced view of the project rather than being limited to statements of deficiencies. Follow-up audits should be conducted to ensure that corrective actions have been implemented satisfactorily.

End product reviews

The technical quality of a project as a whole is determined by the quality of its end products. The basic quality control mechanism for most tasks is the review. Therefore every end product needs to be reviewed in an appropriate manner.

Reviews must be formally documented, with all corrective actions clearly recorded. They are not complete until all corrective actions have been undertaken and checked. Review documentation is essential evidence of quality control and must be retained for the duration of the project. There are three main types of end product reviews used in software, Inspection, Walkthrough, and Review.

- *Inspection.* This is the lowest level of review, appropriate for end products which are small in terms of effort to produce, and are expected to be free of any ambiguous requirements . An inspection usually means that a peer of the author checks the work against its task definition for completeness, against standards for conformance and, as appropriate, for accuracy.

- *Walkthrough.* This procedure is conducted at an intermediate level of formality. It is the most appropriate review technique for end products,

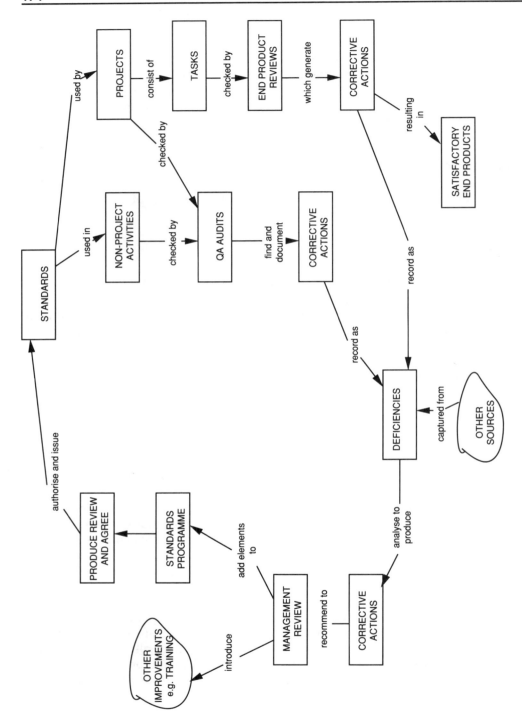

Figure 9.2 A view of the quality management system [Cro 90]

which are medium in terms of effort to produce and relatively free from the possibility of ambiguity in requirements. The author supplies copies of the material to reviewers, who must have some time to familiarise themselves with the material before the walkthrough. The author then leads the meeting and 'walks through' the end product with the reviewers. The object is to ensure that the whole end product is addressed at a reasonable level. The reviewers check the work against its task definition for completeness, against standards for conformance, and, as appropriate, for accuracy.

- *Reviews.* This is a formal procedure and is the most appropriate technique for end products which are at a high level of abstraction or cover a wide area and are open to the possibility of ambiguity in requirements. Reviews consist of two stages. The first stage is a paper review to remove obvious faults and ambiguities. The second stage is the formal review meeting. The meeting is controlled by a moderator, who agrees the venue and time with all participants and ensures that all documents for review are distributed in good time. Reviewers (who may adopt specific roles, such as maintainer) are expected to be properly prepared, which involves checking that the material:

  - addresses correctly and completely all requirements in its precursor,

  - does not introduce new requirements/facilities other than those necessary to satisfy its precursor,

  - is unambiguous and concise,

  - contains sufficient detail (but no more) too allow its successor to be produced to the same criteria,

  - is internally consistent,

  - complies with standards.

Within the review session the moderator has complete control. All other members are equal and 'parliamentary privilege' applies so that people can speak freely, which is essential if the review process is to be fully effective. Reviews are intensive and disciplined and should not exceed two hours.

System deficiencies and corrective actions

Corrective actions recorded at QA audits and reviews relate to errors and deficiencies. In many cases, particularly with reviews, these are specific items which can be corrected locally. Some of the deficiencies, however, are attributable to errors or omissions in the quality system. One activity within the quality system is to capture this information along with other requests for changes to standards and to see that these changes, if required, are implemented.

Management review

Periodic reviews of the quality system are the key to its continued relevance and value. They are also a mandatory requirement to satisfy ISO 9000. The main characteristics of such reviews are:

- They consider all aspects of the quality systems in operation (e.g. do the end products satisfy demand and to what extent does the quality system help?).

- They result in specific improvement actions generally, but not exclusively, resulting in changes to standards.

Standards programme

Projects and activities have lifecycles which differ from those of standards. Standards, either general or local, in a particular area may not exist in a satisfactory form at the time projects commence. They may also change during the life of a project. A list of most current major software standards will be found in reference [SW89].

In order to prevent problems it is recommended that projects produce quality plans which will, among other things, define procedures where suitable standards are not available, and define the standards and versions applicable.

The need for standards has been recognised for many years. Some of the earliest standards were the cubit, inch and metre. Within the software industry the need was recognised and led to the production of many standards [SW89].

Standards are, or at least should be, living relevant documents, that document the best current practice. To achieve this within the quality system there needs to be an ongoing programme of standards production, review and improvement. The following points are taken from a good standards policy and give a good indication for what is required:

The standards programme will be based on taking advantage of the best existing practices in cases where these are documented or otherwise well understood and communicated.

Local standards must be, and be seen to be, produced, reviewed and agreed by practitioners. This will help with user buy-in to them.

Authorisation must be appropriate for the standard, i.e. standards must be perceived as having the support of a relevant authority.

Distribution must match the need, so that everyone who needs to use a standard can do so easily and with minimum effort or risk of using the wrong version.

Procedures for making changes to standards must be readily accessible, easy to use, and users must see that changes they require are evaluated properly and incorporated when appropriate.

Documents not otherwise being changed should be explicitly reviewed and the review documented on a regular basis.

There should be a formal controlled mechanism whereby urgent changes can be communicated and implemented rapidly. Also whereby such changes can be incorporated into the formal system in a more relaxed timescale.

All documents which describe the department's policy, procedures, or standards must state clearly their purpose and scope in a way which is obvious to the reader. They should be seen to help.

We have described the process of managing a quality system—now for the pitfalls.

9.3 THE COMMON PITFALLS OF QUALITY

Many QMS systems and TQM implementations fail. The definition of failure is that the system does not lead to improvement in quality. The usual reasons for failures, as stated earlier, are not technical but people-related as listed below and discussed in this section.

- No demonstrated management commitment.
- No user buy-in.
- Wrong people in the Quality Team.
- QMS too big and bureaucratic.
- Poor communication.
- No perceived added value.
- Complacency and fear of change.
- Lack of appropriate training.

No demonstrated management commitment

This is usually quoted as no senior management commitment. This hides a major problem. Usually senior management are committed. They see a need, as do the staff at the coal face, and who want to work in a quality way. The real problem can be middle management who do not have the time and see the QMS as being not relevant to their day to day problems. Commitment to quality has to demonstrated not just by commitment of resources but also by action. Demonstration of this commitment will help the rest of the team to buy in to the QMS.

No user buy-in

If a QMS is to succeed it must show a benefit for all the users. This benefit will depend upon the user viewpoint. The man or woman hacking the code will see benefits in doing it in a controlled manner providing there is not too much bureaucracy. The senior management will appreciate the control and description of the work. The advantages to middle management will be a combination of these two but will require input and participation.

One of the best ways of ensuring buy-in is to get the user to produce a part of the system or at least be involved in the review. The key to getting user buy-in is to look for small victories to begin with. These must show a quick return to the users; the object is to leave them with a warm feeling about quality.

Wrong people in the quality team

From the previous chapter, you will see that the installation and maintenance of a QMS will require it to be actively pushed and sold. To succeed you need to be a 'quality zealot'. If you want an easy life, stay out of the quality team.

QMS too big and bureaucratic

The size of documentation required to run a QMS can vary from one thin volume to a couple of yards on a shelf. As the system evolves it usually shrinks in size. The question to be answered is: will what we document improve the quality of our product or service? If not, why write it?

Poor communication

Most major problems within projects can be attributed to a failure of communications at some stage The QMS will insist that you will document your contract review and other agreements both with customers and suppliers. This will help to reduce any misunderstandings. Internal communications are also a problem; if the QMS is seen to help and not hinder communications it will help sell the system.

No perceived added value

If the QMS is not seen to help the user or add value to the process, it will not be used. All the staff, from the senior managers to the workers at the coal face, will find reasons for not using the system. This can be a problem both when installing a QMS and when the system has been running for several years. In the early stages the formality and extra documentation are seen as an unnecessary overhead. The key here is to sell the system and keep it simple. Always ensure the documentation really is needed and is seen to add value to the process.

Once the system has been running and is accepted as part of the normal work if it is not seen to change to meet the customer's perceived requirements then the question of added value will again occur. The system must be seen as living and changing to meet the evolving requirements of the user.

Complacency

Complacency and the other side of the coin, fear of change, can be problems for the installation and implementation of quality. The complacency is usually manifested by statements such as 'we are a quality organisation, why do we need a QMS?'. Or 'we have always done it this way and no one has complained'. The same statements are used to mask fear of change. The only way to overcome both of these problems is by showing areas that can be improved and getting buy-in to these improvements. If a new procedure is required get the person it most affects to write it or at least review it.

Lack of appropriate training

One of the major problems with quality is training. One of the American gurus stated 'to get the quality message across, tell them, tell them again and again, and keep on telling them'. This is a simplistic view but the message is correct. You need to invest in training and this investment must be ongoing. This training is the driver for constant improvement.

To help avoid these and other common pitfalls we have produced a checklist for the installation of a QMS. A word of warning, use this and any checklist as an aide-memoire, not a bible—you can miss the important things by using a checklist slavishly.

9.4   A CHECKLIST FOR IMPLEMENTING A QMS

1 Secure senior management commitment:
   ● Don't start until you have it.

2 Appoint someone to project manage the implementation:
   ● Train them.

3 Establish the current state of affairs in the company:
   ● Conduct a survey.
   ● Raise awareness.
   ● Obtain support.

4 Establish the QMS objectives:
   ● Obtain a clear idea of what you want to do—essential in order to measure achievement.

5 Establish organisation and responsibility structure:
   ● Probably exists already but needs formalising.
   ● Establish job descriptions.
   ● Use common format and establish simple review procedure.

6 Agree with line managers the critical functions and activities which need to be procedurally controlled:
   ● Draw flowcharts of activities.
   ● Identify interfaces and critical quality affecting processes.

7 Develop the quality manual:
   ● Design it to ISO 9000 standard.
   ● Keep it short and simple; easy to update and in plain English.
   ● Make it relevant to *your* business.

8 Establish employee participation:
   ● Arrange awareness sessions—little and often is better than one 'sheep dip'.

9 Prepare procedure/work instruction:
   ● Adopt a simple standard format.
   ● Get the users to write and 'own' them.
   ● Keep them short and simple.
   ● Use diagrams and flowcharts.
   ● Remember the skills of the workforce—don't write unnecessary instructions, only those that add value to the process.

10 Implement the system:
- Launch and begin to keep records.
- Establish regular reviews during the early phases to improve untested procedures.
- Appoint and train the auditors.
- Commence the audit programme.

9.5   WHERE NEXT?

There has been very little emphasis on software in this and the previous chapter as most of the items described are applicable to any product or service. We have chosen to use ISO 9000 as the model as it is currently the most generally used and accepted standard worldwide. Examples of other quality systems are shown in Figure 8.6.

The ISO 9000 standard is a general standard and has in the UK been applied to software by using a series of Quality Assurance Standards (QAS) which, in effect, define the rather woolly words used in the standard. This situation was felt to be unsatisfactory as the QAS was a national and not an international guide to the application of ISO 9001 to software development. A guide has recently been produced and ratified by the International Standards Organisation and has been produced under the confusing number of ISO 9001-3 (note the dash). This covers the development and reproduction of software.

The TickIT initiative from the Department of Trade and Industry (DTI) is a UK government attempt to standardise, within the UK, the quality of third-party certification of software and also the quality of auditors. This initiative will ensure that the standard of the audit and auditor is of a uniformally high quality and will use the ISO 9001-3 as a guide.

The application of TQM is increasing but its penetration into the software field is not yet deep due in the main to the lack of universally accepted software metrics. The importance of software metrics can be summed up in the quote 'what gets measured gets done' [PW82]; the only way to ensure process improvement is by measurement.

Figure 9.3 illustrates a simplified model for process improvement and can be applied to the total process or any part of the lifecycle. First you set the objective which will be dependent on the problem and then go round the loop; this is a basic TQM technique applied to software.

At the beginning, and end, of Chapter 8 we used the quote 'quality is optional, you don't have to survive' from Phil Crosby [Cro80]. This, like most quality information, is derived from the manufacturing industry. We are now beginning to see this effect in the software-rich industries. The type of disasters outlined in Chapter 1 will, in the future, not only cost lives and money; they will be a matter of business survival. We are seeing evidence of this trend in the the 1980s. In the USA, fires in computer rooms resulted,

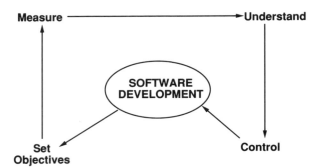

Figure 9.3   A simple process improvement model

within four years, in business collapse in 84% of cases; in the 1990s this crit-
icality will increase. Business will be totally dependent upon software-rich
systems which are not capable of falling back to manual systems. So we
need to improve the reliability and resilience of our systems. The definition
of safety-critical software may need to be reviewed in the light of the above.
A failure may not kill a person but it could be fatal to a business.

The legal aspects of poor-quality software have not yet been discussed
but with increasing reliance on software-rich systems, the lawyers are now
turning their attention to the liability of faulty or off-specification software.

As an example, with the new generation of fly-by-wire aircraft any fault
in the control system could be fatal. If, after an air crash, the black box
recorder indicates a fault that is subsequently traced to the software, who
is liable? The basic interpretation of regulations seems (from a non-lawyer's
point of view) to indicate the supplier who will then have to prove that, at
the time the software was written, every effort was made to ensure the software was produced by state of the art methods. This will mean you must
be able to provide an audit trail through the whole production and testing
lifecycle and be able to show you used the state of the art techniques available at that time. The lawyer's best guess is that this trail should go back
at least 12 years!

This area of litigation would seem to be a money spinner for the lawyers
and a great motivation for software producers to invest in quality. With no
precedence the first cases are going to be critical for the industry. We have
not attempted to see how re-use, re-engineering, maintenance and even
hacking will affect the law. The legal aspect of software alone should justify
the implementation of a QMS if you still need a reason.

9.6   A FINAL POINT

Software is not a science.

It is a technical activity heavily reliant upon people and their organisation.
Unfortunately, most software engineers are intelligent and independent

individuals; hence the quote at the beginning of this chapter that getting them to accept the imposition of a QMS is like trying to herd cats. It is, however, worth the effort, but you must get buy-in from all the QMS system users and that is everyone from cleaner to managing director.

9.7   SUMMARY

Quality systems are procedurally based and, therefore, require documentation and standards, but this documentation must be appropriate to the project in hand and must be seen as helping the user.

The management of software quality is essentially a people issue not a technical one.

Hence most of the pitfalls and problems are due to poor communication. The better the communication within the project, and with both customers and suppliers, the better the quality of the final product.

We are now seeing the production of QMS specifically designed for software. This should provide a baseline for future systems. But always ensure that any such system meets your business needs, not just the requirement of the auditors.

9.8   REFERENCES

[BSI89] *Quality Systems Auditing* BS 7229: 1989 QA (British Standards Institution).

[Cro80] Crosby P.B. (1980) *Quality is Free* (Mentor).

[Cro90] Croucher, K. (1990) *Quality Management System* (Software Quality Mangement Ltd, Milton Keynes).

[PW82] Peters, T.J. and Waterman, R.H., Jr. (1982) *In Search of Excellence* (Harper and Row).

[SW89] Smith, D.J. and Wood, K.B. (1989) *Engineering Quality Software* (Elsevier).

10

Software in the New Decade

*Solemn prophecy...is obviously a futile proceeding, except
in so far as it makes our descendants laugh*

J.B. Priestly (1927)

10.1 INTRODUCTION

All of the previous chapters have concentrated on good practice in software engineering. To complete the picture this chapter looks into the future of this industry and the challenge and requirements of the next decade.

The most immediate challenge of the future in software engineering will be to reduce the time to market of software solutions. There will need to be an increase in the speed of not only development but of innovation as well. If we in the West do not get the process totally under control we will see the Japanese applying their consumer electronics experience to the software industry. The effect could be the same as that of the motorcycle industry described in Chapter 8.

Within ten year's time society will be totally dependent upon an infrastructure that is controlled by software-rich systems. It will be impossible to fall back to manual systems. The implication of this statement is that the availability, reliability and security of these systems will have to be very high.

We have in this book shown that the cost of producing this software, as a proportion of total development cost, has more than doubled in ten years (Figure 10.1). There is no evidence that this trend is slowing down.

In the first chapter we outlined the key stages in software development as a way of introducing the major technical chapters of the book. Chapters 3–7 outline the state of the art in some of the critical areas of software develop-

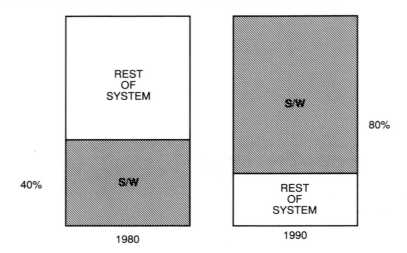

Figure 10.1   Ratio of system/software cost 1980/1990 (Source: DTI)

ment. This only gives you the basic techniques—it is how they are used and controlled that differentiates the winners from the losers.

If the software industry is to meet the challenge of the new decade it will have to improve its act not by just using the best available techniques and implementing new technology but by improving the process of development. The object of this improvement will be to speed the downstreaming of software products and ensure they contribute to meeting the customer's perceived requirements.

The way we control the implementation of new software technologies and the software process is by project management. The link between project, quality and financial management is discussed at the end of Chapter 8. Essentially they are just different ways of looking at the same problem of 'how to supply a product that fulfils the business need of the customer?'. Or putting it another way: what are the risks of not meeting the customer's perceived requirements, be they financial, cost or quality? Let us look at today's project management with all its problems.

10.2   PROJECT MANAGEMENT

In this book we have not discussed the management of the software projects in any depth. There are more than enough project management tools, methods and methodologies available to the software engineer. The basic problem is that all these tools, etc. are based on systems that were originally used in civil engineering. If you take, for example, the building of a bridge over a river, then the problem is well understood, i.e. we need to reduce the time it takes to get from A to B. The process consists of finding a number of solutions to known problems, i.e. count the number of vehicles using the road, make an allowance for increased usage and work out how many lanes you will need. The material used in the construction will be set by cost or esoteric considerations. Once this information is gathered, you then cost the process and set up a project plan to cope with any minor changes, building in a contingency to ensure that the cost of any changes can be met. This process is now under control as you would expect, in an industry, with over 8000 years experience in bridge building.

The software industry is 35 years old. Our customers' problems are usually within their business process for which we provide technology-driven solutions. How often do we really understand the customers' requirements? Or for that matter how often do customers fully understand their own needs at the start of the project? Yet we provide solutions (usually in the form of a fixed price contract) based on the project management and costing methods used by civil engineers. To extend the analogy, look at two instances where the civil engineers got it wrong.

The Tacoma Bridge collapsed when wind blowing up the river moved the bridge and set up resonant oscillations which were not damped by the weight of the structure.

Nearer home the building of the M25 motorway, should have been a quick method of circumventing London. Due to not taking into account that local traffic would use it as a short cut, it has at times become, much to the author's annoyance, 'the largest car park in the world'.

In the software industry we work with the same, if not larger, quantity of unknowns on virtually every project. Therefore, it should not come as a surprise when we are usually late and over budget on our developments. Software project management must be regarded as a less well developed and therefore a risky discipline. We cannot adequately manage software without acknowledging these risks.

A method of controlling these risks is by risk-based project management. This is outlined below.

10.3   RISK-BASED PROJECT MANAGEMENT

Risk management is a whole lifecycle activity (Figure 1.5). It is an integral part of good project management. It is the process of assessing and controlling project risks in order to minimise the chance of disaster, rework costs and schedule overruns and to maximise the chance of completing the project in a quality manner. Where innovative software differs from, for instance, civil engineering is that it is very highly innovative and the old adage is still true that 'you cannot have innovation without risk'. Therefore risk is endemic in software engineering. The best way to avoid the pitfalls of the older project management systems is to get all the parties involved to step back and look at the big picture of the risks and maintain a view throughout the whole project. This will help to avoid the project being blown off course.

The risk management process can be broken down into two main phases each consisting of three steps:

1 *Risk assessment* consisting of risk identification, analysis and prioritisation.

2 *Risk control* consisting of risk management planning, risk response or resolution, and risk monitoring.

The risk identification and analysis activities should involve as many different viewpoints on the project as possible in much the same way as the RCA method described in Chapter 4. Typical viewpoints would be project management, bid management, commercial/finance, sales, analyst/designer, quality, maintenance/support. Identification techniques tend to rely on brainstorming, with or without the aid of checklists of generic risk areas to be considered. Analysis consists of estimating the likelihood of occurrence, and the potential impact on the project, of each risk. Figure 10.2 illustrates this process.

Getting this far in the risk management process has real benefits, in that it raises the project personnel's awareness of potential risks. This enables them to recognise and respond more quickly to situations which indicate that particular risks are becoming more (or less) likely to occur. This contrasts with a rigid plan which can be overtaken by events. It also gives them a sense of being involved in the project and it also improves buy-in by having their individual views taken into account.

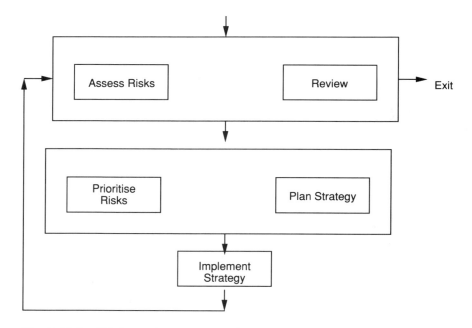

Figure 10.2   Risk-based management

However, risk identification and analysis are not sufficient steps in themselves to enable the effective management of risk.

One of the problems encountered in the risk identification activity is that it tends to produce a large number of risks—too many to be dealt with effectively all at once. The risk prioritisation activity is aimed at discovering which of these risks offer the greatest threats to the project so that management effort can be directed at resolving those risks first. Prioritisation is very much an issue for the project manager, who is in the ideal position to assess the risks. Techniques such as those described in Chapter 4 can help in the systematic proritisation of risks.

Only once a prioritised list of risks is compiled can the project manager start controlling them. This is achieved by deciding on actions to be taken to minimise (or even eliminate) each risk and planning for when these actions should take place by, for example, incorporating them into the project plan or in a contingency plan to be activated at some designated point in the future.

The monitoring aspect of risk control essentially involves going through the entire process again, reviewing the status and priority ordering of risks already identified, identifying new risks, reassessing contingency plans, etc. Risks should be monitored/reviewed on a regular basis but there may also be some events, such as the loss of a key member of the development team, which would trigger a review of project risk immediately.

The benefits of risk-based project management are realised throughout the life of the project as plans are available in advance to deal with risks so that last minute replanning is not necessary. 'Crisis management' and 'firefighting' do not become the order of the day. As existing and new risks are regularly reviewed throughout the life of the project, documentation is available to track major risks and enable all levels of management to see what plans or procedures are to be adopted, and why and when.

In many cases it is possible to identify risks at the project's inception but all to often an optimistic view is taken and risks are overlooked or ignored. This can lead to an unrealistic estimate and proposal or tender being submitted to the customer. The customer may or may not be aware of the risks. He can assume the proposer is aware of the risks or assume that the proposer is naive but also sees an opportunity to have the proposer accept the liabilities. With major contracts the customer may expect to see an assessment of the risks, in an attempt to ensure that the bidder is aware of the risks and can genuinely offer a realistic solution.

Through identifying and reviewing risks it is possible to prepare for (and fund) contingencies. It will be easier to draw on expertise from outside the project team (including that of the customer) if the need for it is identified in advance. By formally agreeing with your customers the probability of risk to the project you inevitably improve communiciations and move closer to them. This is one of the main ideas behind TQM: hiding problems is in no-one's interest if you want repeat business from your customers. This is also one way of ensuring you start to meet all of the customer's perceived requirements.

10.4   QUALITY IN THE FUTURE

We have already defined quality as meeting the customer's perceived requirement. In order to manage and meet this quality requirement we will have to ensure quality is built in and not bolted on as is often the case today. But we have no measures of software quality at present that will stand up to a rigorous engineering approach. This is not surprising as we are trying to measure the customer's perceptions of the product.

The indicators we have used here are the Non-Functional Requirements (NFRs) of the system as these are what the customer perceives as quality. The use of NFRs leads you towards meeting all the customer's functional requirements; if you do not, you will not stay in business. The NFRs can be defined as the qualities of the required system rather than its function; typical examples are performance, usability and availability. They are, in effect, a measure of how well the techniques introduced in Chapters 3–8 are applied. The remaining question is: how do we measure, for example, the NFRs we referred to in Chapter 1? Taking the example of maintainability, this is difficult to express in measurable terms as its definition, ease of maintenance of a system, is too broad. A valid approach is to decompose into its constituent parts of repairability, enhanceability and extendability (Figure 10.3).

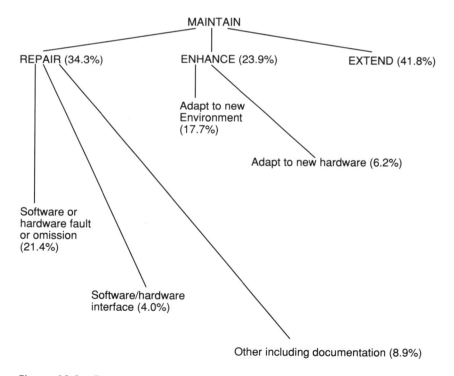

Figure 10.3   Decomposition of NFRs

It is now possible to express these more restrictive definitions in terms of the time, effort or cost to perform the associated well defined tasks. For example, repairability can be defined as the mean time or average cost of repairing a fault. A similar technique can be used for other NFRs. The figure attempts to show the main problem of meeting the customer's perceived requirement—that they change throughout the life of the project. As we stated earlier, we usually agree a delivery time and price before we have fully understood the customer's business problem. This leaves the customer's expectations, which usually rise throughout the project, unfulfilled by the final delivery but with the supplier claiming it meets the agreed specification (usually correctly)! The supplier gets paid for this job, but will he get the next?

Focusing on the NFRs can be used to help manage the customer's expectations (see Figure 10.4). The idea here is that you use Figure 10.5(a) as early as possible in the project, and then throughout, to ensure the customer gets what he wants. Also that any changes in expectations are flagged to the project team so that, when the product is delivered, it meets his perceived requirement. For example, if the torpedo development outlined in Chapter 1 had considered usability more, the captain may still have had his ship intact. A risk-based management approach may have spotted this potential mismatch between what was delivered and its required function.

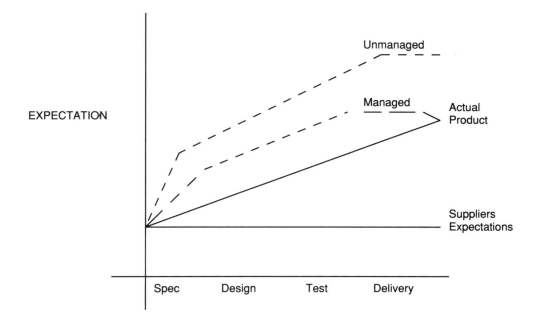

Figure 10.4 Managing customer expectations

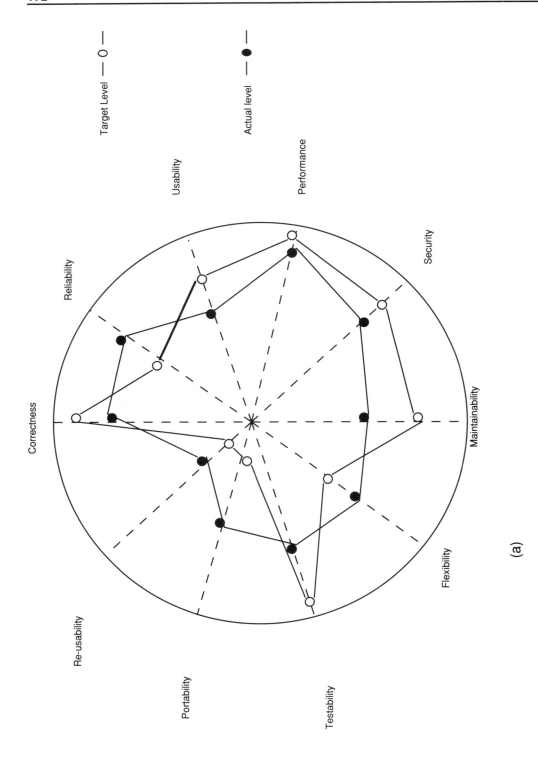

Figure 10.5(a)   Quality characteristics model

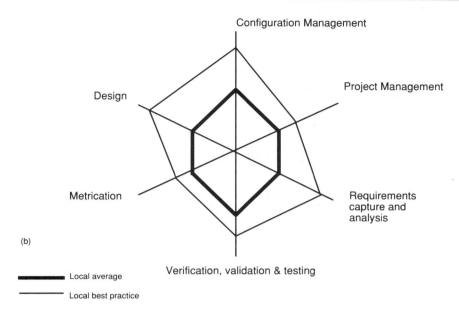

Configuration Management

Project Management

Design

Metrication

(b)

Requirements
capture and
analysis

Verification, validation & testing

■■■■ Local average

—— Local best practice

Figure 10.5(b)   A software process measure

The use of NFRs also has the advantage of validating the requirement throughout the project and improving communication to the customer as well as within the project. The early measure of the NFR may be soft i.e. an opinion, but may still have value in the project and the managing of the customer's expectations.

A problem with the use of NFRs to maximise customer satisfaction is that there is usually a trade-off of one against another. Figure 10.4 illustrates good management of customer expectations.

10.5   THE QUALITY DRIVERS

The two previous sections have looked at minimising risk and at customer-based measure of quality. A final driver for the future is likely to be productivity. This is essential in reducing the time to deliver software.

Productivity is very much reliant upon people, a point stressed several times so far in this book. The prospect of a shortage of good software engineers and the increasing demand for software systems reinforces this point. There is no evidence that this will change in the near future: due to the demographic shift in the West, we will need to increase productivity of both software production and maintenance.

The implementation of a quality system will help (as shown in Figure 1.4) but the best way to improve productivity is to use the best people and process and you only get the best people by careful selection and ongoing training. Training ensures that you are continually improving your most important (and expensive) asset, your people . As we said earlier, software development is innovative and for the forseeable future only people are innovative. A method of ensuring that you are using the best process is by comparing your process against an international standard such as the SEI software maturity model or by comparing yourself against a local best practice check, such as the technical health check shown in Figure 10.5(b). Typical results are shown in Figure 10.5b. The people-related and management problems of software contain enough challenges to fill a book. We do not have the space but strongly recommend *Quality Without Tears: The Art of Hassle-free Management*, by Philip B. Crosby, as a starting point; it is not aimed specifically at software but contains some insights into the problems of this industry.

Figure 10.6 pulls together the key drivers introduced in the last few Sections. This shows the three keys to Total Quality Software—people, process and product. If all three were fully understood, software development would be a controlled, scientific process. This is currently not the case but there are some important pointers towards that ideal in the diagram. The intersection of process and product is the aim of risk-based project manage-

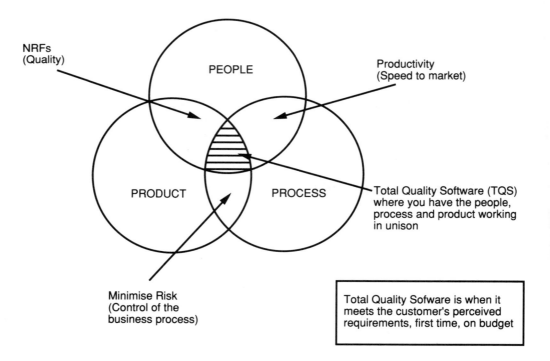

Figure 10.6 Towards TQS

ment—ensuring that the business process of delivering a relevant product is controlled. The area of overlap between people and product is all about focusing the suppliers on what the customer really wants. It is the non-functional requirements described here that give a sustainable quality metric. Finally, the overlap between people and process is all about speed to market. To achieve benefit, a QMS must account for the people who use it.

The ultimate aim in Figure 10.6 is to show the key ingredients of producing software that meets all of the customer's requirements, on time, to budget. Total Quality Software—right first time, every time.

10.6 FINALE

This book has tried to outline the key stages of the techniques and activities that need to be carefully considered in producing software that is fit for purpose—quality software.

Just as we began with a set of cautionary tales of software-based projects, we end with a further one:

During a routine passenger flight, the two pilots were discussing exactly how the engine control circuits of their plane were designed. One thought that the automatic throttle would read engine speed directly from the engine and the other thought it was read from the cockpit panel display. They settled their argument by simply disconnecting the panel display. This action set in frame a dramatic sequence of events.

The panel was in fact the source for the auto throttle—now that it had been disconnected the assumption in the system was that the engine power had fallen to zero.

Immediately the power to the engine was boosted and within one second this power boost caused the compressor blades to stall. This caused hot air to come out of the front of the engine, which in turn, caused an oscillation in the front set of fan blades which struck the cowling and started a fire. Within two seconds one of the blades had broken off, come out of the engine on the blast of hot air, gone through the fuselage and depressurised the cabin.

It is arguable where the blame for this dramatic system failure lies, but several points are clear.

Firstly, the error was not in one implementation. It could have been picked up:

- if the user requirements had been clearly identified;

- if the design notation used had made a very critical input obvious;

- if appropriate tests had been carried out;

- if the potential risk had been identified at any point in the project.

Secondly, it was not the function of the system that was deficient. One of the non-functional requirements—usability—was (or should have been) the central concern.

The increasing reliance on software illustrated throughout this book indicates the need to apply (technical) good practice across the whole life of a software system. Also the importance of adequately addressing non-functional requirements becomes crucial. This applies not just to safety-critical systems but also to telecommunications, data processing and IT systems where competitiveness will be (increasingly) strongly linked to quality: systems of similar functionality will be differentiated on speed to market and satisfaction of NFRs.

This book has focused on these areas. On the technical side we have outlined the key issues and techniques in the vital stages of requirements capture, system design, testing and maintenance. In each of these areas, the aim has been to highlight the most important considerations rather than give details of specific methods. The thinking behind this is debatable—that software technology, as it is, is now adequate. It is its application that needs to move forward.

The remainder of the book has looked at quality. First from a general point of view, then with reference to existing quality control standards and, finally, as an integral part of software development.

Finally, let us recall the Bruce Bond quote with which we opened this text: 'There are only two commodities that will count in the 1990s. One is oil and the other is software. And there are alternatives to oil.' As this, inevitably, comes to pass, best technical practice and a focus on quality will be the differentiators between success and oblivion.

Glossary

The definitions given here are intended to help clarify some of the main text. They are not formal definitions, rather an explanation of terms in the context of this book.

Abstraction A representation of something that contains less information than the something. For example, a data abstraction provides information about some object in the outside world without indicating how the data is represented in the computer. Abstraction is useful in modelling the real world without introducing too much confusing detail. The key to successful abstraction is knowing what to include and what to leave out.

Ada A programming language, developed by the US Department of Defence, specifically oriented to support modern software development practices. Ada purports to provide support for reusable code.

Algorithm A finite set of rules giving a sequence of operations for solving a specific type of problem (e.g. the algorithm for calculating an employee's take-home pay).

Application The user task performed by a computer (such as making a hotel reservation, processing a company's accounts or analysing market research data).

Applications software The software used to carry out the applications task.

Artificial intelligence Software that displays 'intelligence'; e.g. works on the problem of creating programs that can make reasoned judgements. AI applications appear to function as if they were being carried out by a human being.

Assembler A program, usually provided by the computer manufacturer, to translate a program written in assembly language to machine code. In general, each assembly language instruction is changed into one machine-code instruction.

Assembly language A low-level programming language, generally using symbolic addresses, which is translated into machine code by an assembler.

Assessor A person who is qualified and authorised to perform all or any portion of a quality system assessment. There are a number of companies in the UK and Europe who can certify an assessor to carry out audits (e.g. to ISO 9000).

Bug An error in a program or a fault in equipment.

Build The construction of a configuration from its components is called a 'build'.

COBOL A programming language oriented toward business data processing.

Code A set of program instructions. There are many forms of code—see Chapter 2.

Compiler A program which translates a high-level language program into a computer's machine code or some other low- level language. Each high-level language instruction is usually changed into several machine-code instructions. It produces an independent program which is capable of being executed. This process is known as compilation.

Computer A piece of hardware that can store and execute instructions (i.e. interpret them and cause some action to occur).

Configuration A collection of items that bear a particular relation to each other (e.g. the data configuration of a system in which classes of data and their relationships are defined).

Cross compiler A program, written for one computer, which compiles a program written for a second computer, usually a smaller one such as a microcomputer, and outputs appropriate machine-code instructions suitable to be executed on the second computer.

Data Usually the same as information. Sometimes information is regarded as processed data.

Data design The design of the data structure needed by a particular software system.

Debugging The detection, location and correction of bugs.

Design (n) A plan for a program or piece of software.

Design (v) To create a design; to plan.

Development A set of activities that are carried out to create a piece of software (e.g. design, programming, and testing).

DoD   US Department of Defense.

DTI   UK Department of Trade and Industry.

Editor   A program which enables the user to inspect and alter his program or data.

Engineering   A process of applying scientific and other information in specific ways to achieve technical, economic, and human goals.

Error   A fault or mistake causing the failure of a computer program or system to produce expected results.

Evolution   Changes to a piece of software after its initial development; typically, this is repair of problems, adaptation to new conditions, and enhancement with new functionality.

Fifth-generation systems   Computer systems being researched and designed to embody artificial intelligence.

Fourth-generation systems   Computer systems, available and being developed, to introduce higher levels of automation into a range of processes, including the production of software.

Function   A special duty or performance of a thing or a person (e.g. the function of the programmer is to create programs; the function of a compiler is to translate programs from one language to another).

Hardware   Computer equipment, as opposed to the software.

High-level programming language   A problem-oriented language in which instructions may be equivalent to several machine-code instructions, and which may be used on different computers by using an appropriate compiler.

Implementation   The process of converting the notation used to express detailed software design into the program code (also known as coding or programming). Implementation also denotes the task of bringing together the various systems components to get the system working (also known as commissioning).

Interface   The boundary between two things, typically two programs, two pieces of hardware, a computer and its user, etc.

Interpreter   A program which translates and executes a source program one statement at a time.

ISO 9000   A quality system specification for design, development, production, installation and servicing.

Language   An agreed-upon set of symbols, rules for combining them, and meanings attached to the symbols that is used to express something (e.g. the Pascal programming language, job- control language for an operating system, and a graphical language for building models of a proposed piece of software).

Lead assessor   An assessor who is qualified and is authorised to manage a quality system assessment.

Lifecycle   The sequence of states or phases, from requirements analysis to maintenance, involved in software development.

Low-level programming language   A machine-oriented language in which each program instruction is close to a single machine-code instruction.

Machine-code instruction   One which directly defines a particular machine operation and can be recognised and executed without any intermediate translation.

Maintenance   The task of modifying (correcting, updating, etc.) a software system after it has been put into operation.

Method   A systematic approach to tackling a task. Software design methods such as Yourdon and SSADM provide a common approach to design.

Model   An abstraction of reality that still bears enough resemblance to the object of the model that questions about the object can be examined.

Modelling   Simulation of a system by manipulating a number of interactive variables; can answer 'what if...?' questions to predict the behaviour of the modelled system. A model of a system or subsystem is often called a prototype.

Modularisation   The splitting up of a software system into a number of manageable sections (modules) to ease design, coding, etc.

MoD   UK Ministry of Defence.

Object program   The translated versions of a program that has been assembled or compiled.

Operating system   An advanced form of control program which allows a number of programs to be run on the computer without the need for operator intervention.

Phases   Individual stages of work on a piece of software (e.g. the testing phase).

Procedure   A method or set of steps defining an activity.

Process   Technically, a procedure that is being executed on a specific set of data; more generally, a procedure for doing something that is actually being carried out.

Processor   That part of a computer capable of executing instructions. More generally, any active agent capable of carrying out a set of instructions (e.g. a transaction processor for modifying a database).

Product   Usually, an entity to be sold; more generally, the result of some process.

Program   A set of instruction for a computer, arranged so that when executed they will cause some desired effect (such as the calculation of a quantity or the retrieval of a piece of data).

Programming language   An artificial language constructed in such a way that people and programmable machines can communicate with each other in a precise and intelligible way.

Project management   The systematic approach for analysing, organising and completing a project, of whatever type.

Prototype   A scaled-down version of something, built before the complete item is built, in order to assess the feasibility or utility of the full version.

Quality assessment   A systematic and independent examination to determine whether quality activities and related results comply with planned arrangements and whether these arrangements are implemented effectively and are suitable to achieve objectives.

Quality assurance   All the activites and functions concerned with the attainment of quality; it includes the determination and assessment of quality.

Quality control   The practical means of securing product or service quality as set out in the the quality plan.

Quality plan   A document derived from the quality programme setting out specific quality practices, resources and activities relevant to a project.

Quality surveillance   The continuing monitoring and verification of the status of procedures, methods, conditions, processes, products and services, and the analysis of records in relation to stated references to ensure that specified requirements for quality are being met.

Quality system   The orginisational structure, responsibilities, procedures, processes and resources for implementing quality management.

Quality system standards   A document specifying the elements of a quality system.

Release   The issue of software after it has been formally validated by design review.

Requirements analysis   The analysis of a user's needs and the conversion of these into a statement of requirements, prior to specification.

Run-time system   The complete set of software which must be in primary storage while a user program is being executed.

Second party assessments   Assessments of contractors/suppliers undertaken on behalf of a purchasing organisation. This may include the assessment of companies or divisions supplying goods or services to others within the same group.

Software   Programs, data, designs for programs, specifications, and any of the other information that is relevant to a particular set of executable computer instructions (either existing or planned).

Software development lifecycle   *see* Lifecycle

Software engineering   The development and use of systematic strategies (themselves often software based) for the production of good-quality software within budgets and timescales.

Source program   The program as written by the programmer using a programming language; it must be assembled, compiled or interpreted before it can be executed.

Specification   A document, at one level in the hierarchy, which describes either requirement or solutions.

Structured programming   An orderly approach to programming which emphasises breaking large and complex tasks into successively smaller sections.

Subsystem   A system contained within a larger system; usually the subsystem can 'stand alone' (e.g. the programming subsystem in a development organisation).

System   A collection of elements that work together, forming a coherent whole (e.g. a computer system consisting of processors, printers, disks, etc.).

System design   The process of establishing the overall architecture of a software system.

Test data   Data used to test a program or flow-chart; as well as the data, the expected results are specified.

Testing   The process of executing software with test data to check that it satisfies the specification. Testing is a major part of validation.

Third party assessments   Assessments of organisations undertaken by an independent certification body or similar organisation.

Tools   Aids (usually software based) for achieving the various phases of the software development lifecycle.

Transformation   A change of one aspect or form of software into another form (e.g. the transformation of specifications for a program into the design of a program that fulfils the specifications).

TQM   The method of achieving total quality of product and services by involving everyone who can affect the quality of the process.

Utility program   A systems program designed to perform a common task such as transferring data from one storage device to another or for editing text.

Validation   The process of checking a specific piece of lifecycle notation, and the conversion from one piece of notation to another (see also Testing).

Variable   The identifier associated with a particular storage location.

Variable type   The kind of data which is identified by the variable (e.g. alphanumeric, integer, floating point). The type may need to be declared when the variable is first used in a program so that adequate storage space is provided.

Verification   The process of proving that a program meets its specification.

Version control   How all the project assets and products including items from vendors and suppliers and tools needed to produce a deliverable item are controlled.

Waterfall   The name for the 'classical' software lifecycle, so named because the chart used to portray it suggests a waterfall.

Bibliography

Each chapter within this book has a brief list of relevant references at the end of it. This bibliography aims to supplement these lists with useful texts that are not directly referenced.

Abbott, Russell J. (1986) *An Integrated Approach to Software Development* (John Wiley and Sons).

Babich, Wayne A. (1985) *Software Configuration Management: Coordination and Control for Productivity* (Addison-Wesley).

Bersoff, E.H., Henderson V.D., and Siegel S.G. (1980) *Software Configuration Management: An Investment in Product Integrity* (Prentice-Hall).

Boehm, B.W. (1981) *Software Engineering Economics* (Prentice-Hall).

British Computer Society (1990) *TickIT, Making a Better Job of Software*.

Brooks, Frederick P. (1975) *The Mythical Man-Month: Essays on Software Engineering* (Addison-Wesley).

Crosby, Philip B. (1980) *Quality is Free: The Art of Making Quality Certain*, Mentor (New American Library).

Crosby, Philip B. (1974) *Quality Without Tears: The Art of Hassle-Free Management* (McGraw-Hill).

Davis, A.M. (1990) *Software Requirements Analysis and Specification* (Prentice Hall).

DeMarco, Tom and Lister, Timothy (1987) *Peopleware* (Dorset House, New York).

Fairley, Richard (1985) *Software Engineering Concepts* (McGraw-Hill).

Gall, John (1975) *Systemantics: How Systems Work and Especially How They Fail* (Pocket Books).

Gause, Donald C. and Weinberg, Gerald M. (1989) *Exploring Requirements: Quality Before Design* (Dorset House, New York).

Glass, Robert L. and Noiseux, Ronald A. (1981) *Software Maintenance Guidebook* (Prentice-Hall).

Grady, Robert B. and Caswell, Deborah L. (1987) *Software Metrics: Establishing a company-wide program* (Prentice-Hall).

Gunther, Richard C. (1978) *Management Methodology for Software Product Engineering* (Wiley-Interscience).

Ishikawa, K. (1979) *Guide to Quality Control*, Asian Productivity Organization, Tokyo.

Jackson, Michael (1975) *Principles of Program Design* (Academic Press).

Jones, Capers (1986) *Programming Productivity* (McGraw-Hill).

Juran, J.F. Gryna and Bingham, R. (1974) *The Quality Control Handbook, 3rd edition* (McGraw-Hill).

Lehman, M.M. and Belady, L.A. (1985) *Program Evolution: Processes of Software Change* (Academic Press).

Lientz, Bennet P. and Swanson, E. Burton (1980) *Software Maintenance Management* (Addison-Wesley).

Luce, D. and Andrews, D. (1990) *The Software Lifecycle*, Butterworth Heineman, London.

McDermid, J. (1991) *Software Engineers Reference Book*, Butterworth Heinemann.

Musa, J.D., Iannino, A. and Okumoto, K. (1987) *Software Reliability: Measurement, Prediction, Application* (McGraw-Hill).

Nasbitt, John (1982) *Megatrends: Ten New Directions Transforming Our Lives* (Warner Books, New York).

PA Computers and Telecommunications (PACTEL), for the Department of Trade and Industry (1985) *Benefits of Software Engineering Methods and Tools*.

Page-Jones, M. (1980) *The Practical Guide to Structured Systems Design*, Yourdon Press, New York.

Peters, Lawrence (1981) *Software Design: Methods and Techniques*, Yourdon Press, New York.

Peters, Thomas J. and Waterman, Robert H. Jr. (1982) *In Search of Excellence* (Harper and Row).

Pressman, Roger (1987) *Software Engineering: A Practitioner's Approach, 2nd edition* (McGraw-Hill).

The STARTS Purchasers' Handbook, (1986) STARTS Public Purchaser Group (with the support of the DTI and NCC).

National Computing Centre (1984) *The STARTS Guide*.

Sommerville, I. (1985) *Software Engineering, 2nd edition* (Addison-Wesley).

Veryard, R., (1991) *The Economics of Information and Systems Software*, Butterworth-Heineman.

Weinberg, Gerald (1971) *Psychology of Computer Programming* (Van Nostrand Reinhold) pp 126–132.

Index